I0415934

Gifts From America

The Remarkable Record of Aid and Assistance the United States Offers the World

By

Cornelius Deasy

© 2003 by Cornelius Deasy. All rights reserved.

No part of this book may be reproduced, stored in a retrieval system, or transmitted by any means, electronic, mechanical, photocopying, recording, or otherwise, without written permission from the author.

ISBN: 1-4107-8797-4 (e-book)
ISBN: 1-4107-8796-6 (Paperback)
ISBN: 1-4107-8795-8 (Dust Jacket)

Library of Congress Control Number: 2003096737

This book is printed on acid free paper.

Printed in the United States of America
Bloomington, IN

1stBooks - rev. 12/02/03

Peace Corps][Marshall Plan][USAID Foreign Disaster

Assistance][Internet][Global Positioning System

Volcano Disaster Assistance Program][NOAA Hurricane

Hunters][Forest Service International][Global

Food for Education][National Renewable Energy International

][National Institutes of Health][Centers for

Disease Control][Agricultural Research Service][NASA][DOE

Office of Science][National Science Found

State Department De-mining Program][Bureau of Refugees and

Migrations][ICITAP][Cospas-Sarsat][

Contents

Direct Aid, Bring in the Experts

Sharing Technology

Research, Source of Future Gifts

The National Aeronautics and Space Administration has a wide variety of research responsibilities including monitoring the health of our common home, the earth.

The DOE, another big research agency, operates 25 laboratories and research centers that range from particle research and nuclear energy to practical engineering.

Founded by Congress to "promote the progress of science" it funds ten thousand grants each year for the kind of research that may have surprising future payoffs.

With a strong, well-funded research establishment the United States produces a majority of the Nobel Laureates in the Sciences, including many from other countries.

Other Gifts from Other Sources

The 160 members of "Interaction" are voluntary non-profit groups who provide a remarkable array of services and humanitarian functions on an international basis.

A Word of Explanation

On that catastrophic day in September, 2001, when the Pentagon in Washington was devastated and those stately Twin Towers in New York vanished instantly in a cascade of ruin, I felt the same anguish, and the same outrage as everyone else in America. What could we have done to deserve such treatment?

We didn't have to wait long for the answer. Voices here and abroad were quick to claim that "You had it coming and got just what you deserved!" As a leading Episcopal cleric later said: "We are loathed, and I think the world has every right to loathe us". At this point the dispute moved to a different arena. At my age responding to a physical blow is no longer an option but if the dispute become a debate about the American character I'm ready. I don't endorse all of our actions or policies overseas or at home. As big and as powerful a nation as we are we must sometimes look like bullies to people in other countries. But a balanced judgment of America must take into account the historical evidence that this country is and has been a generous citizen of the world, a great gift giver. Thus came the first stirring of a resolve to "set the record straight". The result is "Gifts From America"

If you have been happily retired for a long time it is foolish to get involved in an emotional crusade. It is even worse if the crusade involves writing a book. The idea was simple. All the necessary information would surely be on the internet sites of the federal departments and agencies. It would only be necessary to check these sites and record the good deeds we were doing. What a naïve assumption! The few months I had set aside for this project turned into more than year and would still be going if I had not had the good fortune to enlist the help of Joan Foster, M.L.S., as a researcher. She had the ability to ferret out just the kind of material I needed from the obvious government sites plus a bonus of additional material from web sites I didn't know existed.

One problem I quickly encountered was the size and complexity of many federal agencies. Seen close up our government seems overwhelming. To fully cover the benefits the National Institutes of Health alone offers the world at large would require a book in itself. The best this book can offer in such cases is a brief sample of their obvious accomplishments. To dedicated staff members of these federal agencies this may seem like an outrageous oversight but it could not be helped.

The other side of the complexity problem is the nagging suspicion that something important has been missed, that there are other significant programs that should be recognized. If that is true I have no doubt that the people whose work has been ignored will let me know about it. Fair enough.

The purpose of this book is to acquaint American readers with the remarkable variety of gifts in the form of money, food, health services, education, technical assistance and technology the United States freely gives to the world. This is an aspect of America we should be proud of but, sadly, very few people in this country know anything about it. It is unlikely that the book will influence the way other countries feel about us but that is not the point. My fondest hope is that the book, in some measure, will influence the way Americans feel about our country.

Chapter 1
A Generous Country

On September 11, 2001 the people of the United States became painfully aware that there are people in the world who don't like us. They don't like our system of government, our attitudes about religion, and our aggressive business practices. Most of all they dislike our popular culture. This dislike is strong enough to drive some of them to blow up our embassies, attack our naval vessels, damage the Pentagon, and destroy two of America's landmark office towers.

These actions generated a national sense of outrage in this country and a hard determination to even the score. It also left some puzzling questions: why would the deaths of thousands of Americans peacefully at work in the non-military Trade Center Towers be a cause for street celebrations in the Middle East?

What made the shock even worse was the surprising chorus of voices, both here and abroad, insisting that we got just what we deserved. That attack hasn't stopped. The Los Angeles Times, on January 18, 2003, quoted Episcopal Bishop Frank Griswold as saying "We are loathed, and I think the world has every right to loathe us, because they see us as greedy, self-interested and almost totally unconcerned about poverty, disease and suffering."

Could the Bishop be right? Are we all that bad? Are we really defiling the world with our greedy money culture?

On the record, it seems that the Bishop is guilty of not knowing the American people and of not having any idea of the remarkable variety of ways we offer help to countries around the world. Are the tens of thousands of young Americans who have volunteered to spend two years in the Peace Corps to serve in poor nations around the world "greedy and self-interested". Surely the Bishop doesn't mean that. And do the billions of dollars the U.S. Agency for International Development, our National Institutes of Health, and the Centers for Disease Control spend each year fighting poverty and disease around the world indicate that we are "almost totally unconcerned about poverty, disease, and suffering". Of course not. The problem is that the Bishop obviously doesn't know about these programs. That wouldn't be unusual. Very few Americans do.

Surely we have faults. Some aspects of our culture offend many of our own people just as they offend people in other lands. On the other hand we continuously share our bounty with other countries as we have for many years. Sometimes our gifts are absent-minded. We do something for our own benefit and it turns out to benefit people everywhere. At other times we consciously give the best we have to people in need. If we get blamed for the things we do wrong why shouldn't we get credit for the things we do right?

Those beliefs led to the concept of a book that would spell out the ways in which the United States has been a generous member of world society. It seemed simple at first until it became apparent that there is no official list of American "good deeds". There is plenty of public comment about American "bad deeds" but, as a people, we never give much thought to American programs that have been widely beneficial. In fact, we don't even know that many of them exist. With a little research "Gifts from America" could tell of the many contributions we have made, and continue to make, not to impress people in other countries, but to inform ourselves about a record we have every reason to be proud of.

Are We a Stingy Nation?

There is another strong reason that we need to understand what our country offers the world. In addition to the physical and propaganda attack of the terrorists and other detractors we now have an attack on our national character as tightwads and skinflints. That such terms can be applied to the richest country on earth seems ridiculous but you will find them being repeated in the international press and in leading American newspapers. The argument goes like this.

The United Nations Human Development Programme 2002 shows that while the United States currently leads all nations in the amount of money it provides for direct foreign aid to developing countries it ranks near the bottom of the list in the percentage of gross national product it gives. While our total funding tops the list it represents only 0.1 percent of our gross national product. In contrast, Denmark spends 1.06 percent of its gross national product on foreign aid and Norway spends 0.80 percent.

We have to admire the willingness of these smaller countries to dig deep to help poor nations and the numbers are an

3

embarrassment to the United States. But this is far from the whole story. What you will find in this book is an overview of all the activities our government engages in that benefit the world community. You will see that our direct foreign aid program, which in dollar terms is the largest in the world, is only a small part of the benefits we offer. Understanding the gifts the United States offers the world will surely boost your sense of pride in our country.

More Than a Little Research

The idea that "a little research" would set the record straight on American generosity proved to be naïve. The number, variety and scope of Federal activities that benefit the world at large is beyond anything I could have imagined. Since the book title implies that these "gifts" come from the American people as a whole it means, for the most part, that they were paid for with public funds. The exception would be overseas projects carried out by the Non-Governmental Organizations, the NGO's, a group of very active non-profit organizations that most readers may not have heard of. The federal bureaucracy can, in response to a simple query, bury the questioner with an avalanche of data. The National Science Foundation awards almost ten thousand grants per year and has been doing so for years. The National Institutes of Health, our national treasure as well as a treasure for the world, has about thirty five thousand grants active at any time. Taken with the other departments, bureaus, and agencies that in some way produce services, knowledge, and research that

4

benefits human beings generally rather than just Americans, that is a lot to cover.

Each day spent in research confirmed that this was a story worth telling. The merchant in Mombasa who shops the Internet to determine market prices won't give thanks to America for the Internet. He has no idea how the Internet came to be. The Filipino captain of a coastal steamer navigating the waters of the Sulu Sea knows what the Global Positioning System is because he relies on it to tell him his exact position. He knows what it does but he can't possibly know what it costs the United States to put those twenty four GPS satellites in orbit and keep them circling the globe. All over the world people benefit from medical breakthroughs, crop improvements, communications systems, disease control and other benefits that originate in activities funded by our government. It's not surprising that people in other countries don't know where these gifts come from but it is shocking that we as a nation know so little about them. They should be a source of pride for every American.

The information reported here has come directly from open government files that are accessible to anyone. The activities and programs reported and the numbers and dollar amounts given are official. In order to cut the volume down to a manageable level, to focus on real gifts, and to sort the material into understandable categories, some rules had to be established.

What Constitutes a Gift?

In reviewing the activities of our government that offer benefits to other people and other countries it quickly becomes apparent that gift giving comes in different forms. The criterion used in this book is that any activity of the United States Government that produces benefits that are available without charge to other people is a gift. That is a very broad definition that covers a wide range of programs.

- Direct Giving: Handing over something of value to somebody else is a gift by any definition. The United States Agency for International Development which provides money for a wide array of beneficial activities around the world is a large scale direct giver. So is the Department of Agriculture which administers various food aid programs.

- Personal Services: At the request of other governments the United States sends a variety of Americans abroad to help with local problems. These range from members of the Peace Corps to scientists from the U.S. Geological Survey, the Forest Service, the Department of Energy, and the Centers for Disease Control.

- Technology: The Global Positioning system, which makes it easily possible for anyone to know exactly where they are on the surface of the globe, was developed and financed by our government but is available for anyone to use. The same can be said for the Internet, originally developed to connect research laboratories in this country but now used worldwide.

- Providing Information: A variety of government agencies develop and collect data that is available to anyone who needs it. NOAA, the National Oceanic and Atmospheric Administration, with its array of weather satellites and its Hurricane Hunter airplanes provides critical weather information for much of the western hemisphere. It also maintains a library of weather data from around the world that is accessible to anyone. The library of the National Institutes of Health is another world class source of information for the medical field.

- Providing Research: The United States funds a tremendous amount of research in a variety of fields. Evaluating this research as a gift is complicated. The research sponsored by the National Institutes of Health, dealing with health problems of people around the world, is clearly a gift. On the other hand it is hard to see how the deep space exploration programs of the National Aeronautics and Space Administration, conducted purely for the purpose of expanding our knowledge about the universe, is going to be of direct benefit to anyone in our lifetime. Yet pure research, conducted solely to satisfy scientific curiosity without any specific application in mind, has provided the knowledge base for many of the benefits we enjoy today and will probably do the same in the future. On that basis we have to consider the kind of work done in our space program and in our national labs as exploring new fields that will provide gifts of the future.

Sorting the Information

The "gifts" discussed in this book are just a sample. There is much more that is not included because it would be repetitive. The United States Agency for International Development's Program for Promoting Humanitarian Assistance is covered here. It is an extremely important program because it provides direct and immediate humanitarian assistance to people suffering from natural and man-made disasters. However, it is only one of six important programs that USAID carries on overseas. The fact that all of them are not discussed in the same detail may seem unfair but the important point is that the reader understand the nature and scope of USAID's activities rather than read all the details.

In the same fashion the Centers for Disease Control, which conducts very diverse programs, currently has agreements to operate its Global AIDs Program in nineteen countries. It provides both funds and technical assistance depending on the special needs of each country. You do not need to hear the details of each of these programs to understand that the GAP project is a true gift from the American people to other people who face a desperate problem.

In addition to condensing information it has been necessary to reclassify it under a few major headings. This is important because departments and agencies of our government engage in a bewildering mix of activities. The Department of Energy operates some of the world's most famous laboratories for research in particle physics and the nature of matter. It also provides consulting teams to help developing countries harness the sun's energy to bring electric power to remote villages through the use of photovoltaic systems. These two programs range from the outer edge of human knowledge to the simple use of solar energy. Clearly they do not fall in the same category even though they originate in the same Department. Each has been assigned to one of the following categories.

- **Direct Aid, a Legacy of Generosity**

    This category includes a remarkable array of programs ranging from such historic successes as the Marshall Plan and the Peace Corps to multi-billion dollar agencies such as the U.S. Agency for International Development.

- **Direct Aid, Sending in the Experts**

    A group of valuable but little known overseas services offered by our Geological Survey, our Forest Service, and the Department of Energy.

- **Sharing Technology**

The Internet, the Global Positioning System, and The National Oceanic and Atmospheric Administration.

- **Medicine and Public Health**

The National Institutes for Health, the Center for Disease Control and Prevention, and some Star Medical Performers. Other nations support medical research and offer medical assistance to other countries but not at this scale.

- **More Food for Everyone**

The United States Department of Agriculture is a big, venerable agency that has been successful in increasing the world's food supply.

- **Research, Source of Future Gifts from America**

The National Aeronautics and Space Administration, the Department of Energy, and the National Science Foundation carry on vast research programs in the sciences that will probably be the source of the next generation's useful gifts. We not only generate a large number of our own Nobel Laureates here, we also nurture many from other countries.

- **NGO's, Gifts From Other Sources**

Non-Governmental Organizations are non-profit, voluntary groups such as the American Red Cross, and CARE, that are devoted to humanitarian activities in other countries. While these agencies may contract with the United States Government to provide specialized services in specific areas for the most part they are funded directly by the American people.

World War II was a starting point for activities and policies that generated many of the gifts described here. The Marshall Plan to assist the democracies of western Europe after the war introduced a concept of direct assistance that became the present United States Agency for International Development. The critical importance of scientists and engineers to the war effort led to the National Science Foundation for supporting research and training in these fields. These programs have produced more than we could have ever hoped for. The NSF particularly has been a major factor in establishing this country as a center of technology.

Selecting the material offered in the following pages has not been a purely objective process. There is too much of it. In dredging through endless pages of research material there is occasionally a rewarding moment when something that is personally irresistible appears and must be included. In fact, the whole process is colored by such choices. Interest is definitely a criterion. Other writers might have come up with different selections but the ones you find here are all solid gifts from America.

Direct Aid, A Legacy of Generosity

Chapter 2
The Marshall Plan

If Americans ever feel the need to search their history for some action that was at once wise, humane and generous, they need look no farther than the Marshall Plan, an astonishingly benevolent and history-making endeavor to aid and re-build a defeated enemy. It was both exceptionally generous and an act of enlightened self-interest.

At the end of World War II, Western Europe was devastated physically, politically, economically and emotionally. The means of subsistence for most people was largely destroyed. Not only did the economy of the countries under foreign occupation lie in ruins there was a real fear that they might sink into chaos, a situation that would benefit no one. In the East, the armies of the Soviet Union had taken a firm grip on the territory it had occupied and there was great concern that they might continue their advance into a weak and disorganized Western Europe.

Speaking at Harvard University in June of 1947, Secretary of State General George C. Marshall announced his proposal for the European Recovery Program, a program that became better known as the Marshall Plan. Recognizing that the physical destruction and the economic disruption were far more serious than realized at first, he proposed that if the nations of Western Europe would devise a

15

program for their own economic recovery the United States would provide the funds to expedite it. The British Foreign Secretary, Ernest Bevin, predicted that Marshall's address "will rank as one of the greatest speeches in world history" Secretary Marshall was not a dynamic speaker but his message was astonishing.

Unless you have seen the damage wrought by heavy aerial bombardment it is hard to visualize the devastation it can cause. Principal military targets, railroads, highway bridges, industrial complexes, and control centers, were gone. But as Marshall said in his Harvard speech, this destruction was not the most important part of the problem.

"In considering the requirements for the rehabilitation of Europe the physical loss of life, the visible destruction of cities, factories, mines, and railroads was correctly estimated, but it has become obvious during recent months that this visible destruction was probably less serious than the dislocation of the entire fabric of European economy. Long standing commercial ties, private institutions, banks, insurance companies, and shipping companies— have disappeared."

In 1948 Congress passed the legislation that created the Marshall Plan. It was not a program that was viewed enthusiastically at first by all parties. The idea that this country, which had just finished an enormously expensive war, should pay the cost of correcting the devastation the countries of Western Europe had brought on themselves didn't seem reasonable. Senator Wherry of

Nebraska said that "sending money to Europe would be like throwing tax dollars down a rat hole."

Two things happened in 1948 that drastically changed the situation: Russian forces took over Czechoslovakia and Russia cut off access to Berlin, a city that was jointly occupied by the Allies. It was this last action that brought on the Berlin airlift. All the food and fuel needed to keep Berliners alive had to be flown in. These actions made it clear that if Western Europe was to defend itself from Russian domination, American help was necessary.

The impact of the Marshall Plan on the countries of Western Europe was remarkable. By the time the Plan ended in 1951 thirteen billion dollars in American aid, over one hundred billion dollars in today's terms, had been given to:

Austria	Belgium	Denmark
France	Greece	Iceland
Ireland	Italy	Luxembourg
The Netherlands	Norway	Portugal
Sweden	Switzerland	Turkey
The United Kingdom	West Germany	

These nations proposed the projects for funding and negotiated with the American authorities for allocations. The activities funded were astonishing, ranging from land reclamation, industrial modernization, and low cost housing to massive hydroelectric projects. In Berlin, Marshall Plan aid provided for the replacement of the main power station that had been dismantled by the Russians as part of reparations. The Limberg Dam was built in Austria, the Corinth Canal in Greece was reopened, and the famous Orient Express, which linked Greece to Western Europe, was restored.

Assistance took many forms. One of the most important was the system set up for the exchange of technical and production information between Europe and the United States. Near the end of the program the Marshall Plan Organization had 370 experts overseas and sponsored 145 productivity teams involving more than 1,000 European labor, management and agricultural representatives. Technical assistance funds were used to conduct seminars for European managers, training programs for European engineers, and distribute technical and scientific information.

After only two years of the plan and less than five years after the end of World War II most of the seventeen countries above had made great strides in rebuilding their economies. Overall industrial production exceeded pre-war levels by fifteen percent. The historic democracies of Western Europe had been saved and the foundation laid for a stronger and more unified Europe.

Economist of the time were agreed that the aftermath of World War I, which lead to trade disruptions and the erection of tariff barriers, was the cause of the word-wide depression of the 1930's They viewed the Marshall Plan as having spared the world a repeat of that dismal period.

A German evaluation of the Marshall Plan used these terms:

"The history of the Marshall Plan remains as astonishing for those who already know it as for those who hear of it for the first time. Briefly, this is how it can be summed up.

The victor of World War II took pains, through generous aid, to prevent starvation among the people in the principal war areas, to eliminate the devastation of those areas as quickly as possible and begin economic reconstruction immediately.

The victor included -not excluded-the former enemy, Germany, in his plan.

He prevented thereby a repetition of the world-wide economic depression of 1929-31.

He laid the foundation, simultaneous with the reconstruction program, for the unification of the countries of Europe and close Atlantic partnership"

Not only did the plan accomplish what it was designed to do, it set a precedent that has affected our policies since that time. It was the forerunner of the United States Agency for International Development which carries on today.

The only criticism leveled at the Plan is that it was so successful that it led to the mistaken assumption that the formula used in reviving Western Europe would be successful anywhere. The past forty years has demonstrated that this is not true. The nations of Western Europe had strong public systems of governance, and strong judicial systems. They had the organizational framework in place to accept the American aid and put it to productive use. When aid has been supplied to other countries without similar traditions and strong public systems the results have often been disappointing.

Before leaving the Marshall Plan we should look at the accomplishments of George Catlett Marshall. A career soldier, he was chief of staff of the United States Army during World War II, playing a critical role in that conflict. Winston Churchill hailed him as "the true organizer of victory". In recognition of his diverse abilities he was later appointed Secretary of State. In 1953 he received the Nobel Peace Prize for his leadership in reviving a shattered Europe. He was a true soldier-statesman.

If ever there was a gift from America that we can be proud of the Marshall Plan was it.

Chapter 3

The United States Agency for International Development

Following the end of the Marshall Plan the United States Government set up a variety of other programs and organizations to continue assistance to nations in trouble but none completely satisfied the need. In 1961 the Foreign Assistance Act was passed and the United States Agency for International Development (USAID) was formed. For the past forty two years it has been this country's principal agency for giving aid to the developing countries of the world.

"U.S. Overseas Loans and Grants", published by USAID, lists the involvements of the agency and its predecessor organizations, principally the Marshall Plan, from 1945 to the year 2000. It reveals an agency that has been active through changing times and changing foreign policy agendas. It has also displayed a considerable amount of financial muscle. During that period of time it distributed $210,330,000,000 in loans and grants. The full measure of American loans and grants, including those made by other agencies, is $364,348,000,000. Translated into current dollars those sums would be vastly greater.

It is surprising to find such prosperous countries as Sweden, Denmark and Norway on the list of countries receiving grants but this occurred when western Europe was recovering from the devastation of World War II. France and Great Britain were big beneficiaries of this aid, receiving $3,199,600,000 and $3,835,500,00 respectively.

Since that time the list of beneficiaries has changed greatly. Many of the countries that receive help from USAID, countries like Burkina Faso, the Kyrgyz Republic, Cape Verde, Lesotho, and East Timor, would be hard for most people to locate on the map. Major targets for assistance have switched from the Western European nations of the Marshall Plan to India, Pakistan, and Turkey. India leads this group with $5,407,800,000 in grants and loans. The smallest is Samoa which received two book-mobiles worth $24,000.

What makes it difficult to determine what money went where and why are the myriad special programs Congress has approved to deal with special problem areas of the world, such as Assistance for the Independent States of the Former Soviet Union, and Assistance to Portuguese Colonies in Africa.

USAID is a big agency with a big, complicated program. It currently operates on a budget of over eight billion dollars with field missions in 72 countries and programs in more than 100. Overall foreign policy guidance is provided by the Secretary of State. USAID's mission is to "support the people of developing and transitional countries in their efforts to achieve enduring economic and social progress". In pursuing those goals it has been, and is, of great benefit to developing countries around the world. It has clearly been a gift from America, but in a variety of ways rather than in a single focused program.

The Agency has six strategic goals:

1. Encourage economic growth and agricultural development;

2. Strengthen democracy and good governance;

3. Build human capacity through education and training;

4. Stabilize world population and protect human health

5. Protect the environment for long-term sustainability;

6. Promote humanitarian assistance.

That list should convince you that USAID has taken a very ambitious bite at world problems.

Evaluating the success of USAID in meeting many of these goals is difficult. The one that is easiest to measure, and at the same time most encouraging to consider, is promoting humanitarian assistance. It is also more important than you would imagine. Globally, almost two billion people were affected by disasters during the 1990's. In 1999 alone disaster affected 212 million people and caused more than seventy-two billion dollars in damages. And these are only natural disasters. In the same year 27 major armed conflicts in 25 countries uprooted more than 35 million people worldwide. Fourteen million people are refugees outside their home countries and 21 million others are displaced within their own country. Humanitarian assistance is a critical need around the globe.

USAID responds to these needs through the Food For Peace Program (FFP) and the Office of Foreign Disaster Assistance (OFDA). They respond to emergencies that are relatively small and highly focused and others that spread over vast areas and continue for years. In doing this they cooperate with both the local governments and other international aid organizations. Here are some examples.

- In November of 2001 violent gales and a deluge of rain lasting over 24 hours hit northern Algeria causing massive mudslides and flood damage. Seven hundred and fifty-one people died, 40,000 people were left homeless and 2,700 buildings were severely damaged by the floods. Within three days the Office of Foreign Disaster Assistance provided a cash payment to the Algerian Red Crescent Society for local purchase of relief supplies for affected individuals. Within a week OFDA was air lifting blankets, medical supplies, heating equipment and generators into the devastated city. Total expenditure within the first two weeks was one quarter of a million dollars.

This was a first response. It was followed by the arrival of staff experts to determine whether additional USAID/OFDA assistance was necessary.

- In January of 2002, Mt. Nyiragongo, in the Democratic Republic of the Congo, erupted sending a major lava flow to the city of Goma, ten miles away. Television pictures of the event showed a wall of black lava slowly moving down the streets of the city while people, backing away from the molten rock, helplessly watched as their homes and businesses were destroyed.

Twelve thousand five hundred households were destroyed and 30,000 people were homeless.

The response to this disaster followed the same sequence seen in Algiers:

immediate cash to local authorities for purchase of relief supplies followed by air lifts of essential personal and community needs. In addition the USAID/Food for Peace Program authorized 1,714 metric tons of food supplies and the U.S. Department of Agriculture added another 3,450 metric tons of food. Total assistance provided by these agencies during this first phase response was $4,278,087.

While natural disasters such as these two are devastating, USAID, in conjunction with other international relief organizations, is equipped to move quickly to meet primary needs. In a secondary phase, it can follow on to assist in long-term reconstruction.

Natural disasters are cruel but helping hands are available. It is the man-made disasters of war that seem endless and intractable. They produce the most casualties and displace the most people and they consume the greatest share of humanitarian relief. Efforts to ease the plight of the people of the Sudan show the difficulty.

- Sudan, a nation in the north-eastern corner of Africa, has experienced an 18-year civil war between the Islamic government of the north and the rebel tribes of the south. An estimated two million people have perished as a result, from fighting, famine, and disease. USAID's Office of Foreign Disaster Assistance has been active in Sudan since 1987, dealing with emergency needs of the war-affected and drought-affected populations directly and also in conjunction with the United Nations program.

In addition to those who have died, 442,500 refugees have fled the southern tribal zone into adjacent countries, the only hope they have of survival—if someone will feed them. While official USAID publications do not touch on all the tragedies that result from the collapse of a society, other sources have reported that the slave trade has reappeared in the devastated south.

The United Nations and other governments are involved in the Sudan disaster along with USAID and other agencies of the United States government. A major effort is getting food and providing medical care in the worst hit districts, and supporting the refugee camps. Total financial assistance to Sudan in 2001 from the United States was $154,704,528. Man-made disasters are expensive.

We could continue this string of disaster reports around the world but the stories would be much the same. In the year 2000 USAID responded to 74 disasters from Afghanistan to Vietnam, including 21 floods, five epidemics, eight cyclones/hurricanes, and three earthquakes. Through its Office of Foreign Disaster Assistance and Food for Peace Program, USAID is a major factor in dealing with humanitarian needs around the globe.

Remember that humanitarian assistance is only one of six strategic goals. Equally encouraging activities are underway in other areas. The variety and scope of the activities USAID supports to improve public health in the developing world is especially impressive.

- USAID programs have resulted in over 50 million couples in the developing world adopting family planning practices. As a result the average number of children born to couples in those countries has dropped by one third.

- Infantile paralysis, virtually eliminated in the United States in the sixties, is now being eliminated in the developing world, having dropped from 350,000 cases per year in the 1980's to 2,400 cases now.

- The Agency's "Boost Immunization" program is pressing to spread the use of immunization to reduce infectious disease. It has recently extended its immunization program to 14 additional countries with low immunization rates.

- Malaria, the leading cause of death for children under five in Benin, is now being controlled due to a new program for distributing the malaria control drug chloroquine. A study funded by USAID and conducted by the Center for Disease Control determined that the primary source of this drug in Benin was a low quality form sold in village markets. Improperly administered, it had the effect of increasing malaria's resistance to the medication rather than curing it. The solution to the problem was to put distribution into the hands of trained community-based health agents who could give proper instructions on its use.

- In El Salvador, USAID is involved in the effort to improve the health of the country's children, especially those living in rural areas. One part of this program is called Healthy Kitchens for Healthy Schools. In order to make that program work you need people who know how to prepare healthy food so classes were established to train local housewives to see that their children got the right nourishment. As one of them said, "This is the first time that someone thinks we can do something worthwhile, that our help is needed."

Education is the road that offers developing nations the best chance of escaping poverty and creating a more prosperous and freer life for their citizens. USAID has been working on education problems for many years.

- USAID education and training programs in Egypt began in 1975. Since then it has funded almost 2000 schools in rural areas with a particular concentration on increasing the attendance of girls. As a result, gender gaps in Egypt have decreased. Statistics show that the number of girls in rural Upper Egypt currently enrolled in primary school continues to rise, having increased 15 percent in the past five years. An interesting part of this program has been a collaborative effort between the Egyptian government and USAID to produce an Egyptian "Sesame Street", helping to prepare millions of Egyptian children for primary education by improving basic literacy and numeracy skills.

- USAID educational efforts in the Himalayan kingdom of Nepal started in 1954. Since there was little in the form of an educational establishment to start from the first program was to train teachers to train teachers. When planning began for the College of Education eight Nepali trainers traveled to the United States on USAID scholarships to prepare to serve as administrators of the new institution. External training of this sort has continued and in the last five decades 5,500 Nepalis have participated in USAID training programs in the U.S., India, Thailand, and the Phillipines.

In 1978 USAID undertook to increase the reach of the teacher training activities in Nepal by instituting a Radio Education Teacher Training service. Regularly scheduled broadcasts supported by self-instructional textbooks bring teacher training services to rural populations that are otherwise difficult to reach in the Himalayas.

The story of Januka Khadka illustrates how useful even a little education can be in some parts of the world. She joined a USAID literacy program in order to learn to sign her name. In fact, she did much more, learning both English and Nepali numbers that equipped her to count money, catch the right bus, and dial a telephone. Compared to our own educational standards that seems like a perilously limited education but this knowledge equipped her to serve as chairperson of the village women's savings and investment group, keeping the personal account books and helping individuals with their personal accounts. That sounds like a big payoff for a limited education.

The examples covered here represent only a small part of USAID's activities on behalf of those parts of the world that are struggling to cope with adversity and improve the lives of their people. The scale of these activities range from the disaster in the Sudan where the cost of support is measured in hundreds of millions of dollars and hundreds of thousands of metric tons of food aid to training village mothers in Salvador to prepare healthy meals for the schools.

This is by no means the sum of USAID's activities. Among those activities that appear where you might least expect them are the Enterprise Development Centers in the Central Asian Republics of Kazakhstan, Kyrgyzstan, Tajikistan, and Uzbekistan. These EDC's are staffed with qualified teams of local and international experts to provide training and guidance to small and medium sized enterprises in these countries in order to stimulate economic growth.

As we will see in later chapters this agency also supplies the funds for other departments of the U.S. Government that provide specialized technical assistance to the developing world. USAID is clearly a major, ongoing supplier of gifts from America tailored to the needs of recipients all around the world.

Chapter 4

The Peace Corps, A Gift of Young Americans

No other program of our foreign aid activities has received the warm public support the Peace Corps has enjoyed. While a shipment of food from America may mean the difference between life and death for the people who receive it, the people who send it never see it. It is just a news announcement. Peace Corps shipments are very personal. We are sending our prize resource, educated young Americans who are highly motivated to make the world a better place. It was a successful program in the beginning and now, forty two years later, it is still a prize.

The idea surfaced during the 1960 presidential campaign. Arriving at the University of Michigan at 2:00 o'clock in the morning, John F. Kennedy was surprised to find 10,000 students patiently waiting to hear him speak. What they heard was the first outline for the Peace Corps. As President, Kennedy described his vision for the program in his inauguration speech: "to those people in the huts and villages across the globe struggling to break the bonds of mass misery, we pledge our best efforts to help them help themselves."

It was a popular idea and things moved swiftly. In March 1961 President Kennedy signed an executive order establishing the Peace Corps. By July assignments were planned for Ghana, Tanzania, Colombia, the Philippines, Chile, and St Lucia and over 5000 applicants had taken the first examinations to enter the Peace Corps.

In August the President hosted a Rose Garden ceremony to honor the first group of Volunteers to leave this country for service in Ghana and Tanzania. For Washington to organize such a complicated mission, train volunteers, and make sensitive arrangements with host countries within a span of six months was an astonishing achievement and a measure of the interest felt in this country.

In September of 1961 Congress formally authorized the Peace Corps to "promote world peace and friendship" through three goals:

1.   To help the people of interested countries in meeting their needs for trained workers

2.   To help promote a better understanding of Americans on the part of the people served.

3.   To help promote a better understanding of other people on the part of Americans.

Two years later 7,000 volunteers were working in the field in 44 countries from Afghanistan to Uruguay.

It is worth remembering what we asked these intelligent, well educated young people to do. Raised in comfort and standing on the threshold of their own careers in their own country we were asking them to turn their back on all they had grown up with and take these two-year assignments. They were not going to the urban centers of Africa, Latin America and Asia. They were going to remote villages to help people living in poverty. Volunteers were expected to live at the level of the co-workers with whom they work and become members of the community in which they live. In many cases they would live in conditions that few of them had ever known, without electricity, running water, or the simplest systems of sanitation. One volunteer described her concrete housing unit as one room with an adjoining bathing space with only a hole in the floor for a drain. There was a flush toilet but no running water. There was a closet size space for cooking but no electricity. Water had to be carried from an outside well.

For all this volunteers were rewarded with a monthly living allowance that covered housing, utilities, personal transport, food, and clothing.

In the years since it was formed more than 165,000 Peace Corp volunteers have served in 135 countries. Assignments of volunteers were made on the basis of the needs expressed by the countries seeking help and the training and skills of the volunteers. In the early days of the program more than half the volunteers served as teachers. Teaching assignments ranged from primary subjects in elementary schools to science, math and English in secondary schools. Some advanced education volunteers helped university level students develop English language skills they needed to go on to specialized studies in medicine, engineering and business.

Health volunteers worked at the grass roots level with local governments, clinics, and communities where health and sanitation needs were most urgent. They concentrated on outreach programs to teach public health, hygiene, and sanitation. They helped to assure clean water supplies, dig new wells, build latrines, and teach communities to maintain them. That is real grass roots work.

Agricultural volunteers filled a variety of niches depending on their specific training. Some conducted work shops on pest management, tested new seed varieties, and demonstrated post-harvest crop treatment. Advanced volunteers worked with farmer cooperatives and agribusinesses teaching basic business practices and cost and price analysis. Volunteers with a background in livestock sought to improve farm family nutrition and income through improved management of farm animals.

In later years this mix changed as men and women with professional skills, such as doctors, engineers and horticulturists, volunteered for service. The age mix also changed. The average age grew to 27 years with five percent of the volunteers over 50. An increasingly capable and dedicated group was being sent overseas to offer American help and friendship to countries in need.

The scope of the program has also been enlarged. A new program to support entrepreneurial activities in business and tourism was developed in 1982. In 1995 the Crisis Corps was formed to allow experienced volunteers to return and provide short-term assistance during natural disasters and humanitarian crises.

While dedicated service was the norm for volunteers there were some that demonstrated leadership and capability that was truly remarkable. Mark Schneider, Director of the Peace Corps, in commenting on the effort that was being put into the fights against AIDS that has devastated much of Africa, tells the story of a single volunteer who developed an exceptional program in the battle against AIDS.

"At the International AIDS Conference in Durban, South Africa, the work of a single volunteer in the Ivory Coast was featured. She had been working in a rural village as a health educator and developed materials in the local language and sensitive to the local culture to explain the epidemiology of the disease and the ways to prevent its spread. She taught her fellow health workers to do the same and then the District Public Health Supervisor asked her to teach all provincial health workers. Her two years were coming to an end but the Minister of Public health asked her to extend for a year to establish a training program, using her materials, to educate all 3,300 health educators in the country on how to prevent the spread of the disease."

Peace Corps volunteer Liz Schuster made her mark in a different way. During her three years of service in Guyana, South America, as a Health Education volunteer she wrote and illustrated seven books featuring "Lolita and Maria", two Amerindian school girls, that addressed critical health issues such as HIV/AIDS, malaria, alcohol, and nutrition in the context of the Amerindian culture. Impressed by her work the Guyana Book Foundation paid for printing copies for distribution to Amerindian communities throughout Guyana.

How do you explain the willingness of so many intelligent, well-educated young Americans to take these two year assignments? They would go to teach classes, to develop water systems, to improve roads, to improve agriculture and animal husbandry, to set up health services, and to offer whatever they could to make life better for the people they came to help. When you read the reports of the returning volunteers you sense a very high order of altruism, a strong feeling that they had something of value to give to those in need and were willing to accept personal sacrifices in order to do it. An unanticipated result of their commitment is that so many returned feeling that the experience had benefited them as well as the people they served. The hope of Congress that the program would be a two-way street has been realized. People of the host countries established a close and affectionate relationship with the Americans and the volunteers leave with a much better understanding of the difficulties of life in the developing world and a deep affection for their people.

Did they feel that they made a difference?

"My parents, who had served as Volunteers in Kenya 25 years before I joined the Peace Corps, had absolutely no idea how much influence they had during their two years of service. They did not consider themselves exceptional volunteers; they simply went to class, taught a variety of subjects in the best way they knew how, and loved the people they lived among. But returning with me to their village so many years later, they were struck by the undeniable realization that they had, indeed, changed people's lives." Tara Elizabeth Beverwyck, Volunteer in Malawi, 1995-98

Did they feel genuine affection for the people they worked with?

"The kids I taught were always with me, and I loved them even more than I once loved my privacy. I always wanted to have children, but I never thought I'd have so many and so soon". Tina Martin, Volunteer in Tonga, 1969-71

Did they bring back memories that sustain them today?

"The rush of pride and sense of awareness I shared with the people I worked with comes back to me at different times during my life today. I think of it when I need a reminder of how humans everywhere contribute each day to the well-being of our world. This happens whether we are recognized for it or not. This lesson is one of the many gifts given to me while I was a Peace Corps Volunteer." Dianne Garyantes, Volunteer in the Dominican Republic, 1989-91.

In preparing this section of the book I called my niece, Jacquelyn Florsheim, who served in the early days of the Peace Corps in West Africa. Just graduated from college she was highly motivated to give what she could to people in need. After first serving in Liberia she was so committed that she signed on for two more years in Sierra Leone. Her memories of her experience are still bright. The ability of the people they came to help to remain normal and cheerful in the face of severe survival conditions amazed all the volunteers. In her words, "I brought back far more than I took with me. They changed my life."

How well has the Peace Corps performed during the past forty years? A program that has involved 165,000 men and women serving in 135 countries in a wide variety of activities is not easy to evaluate. The best simple evaluation is that the fact that new countries continue to request Peace Corps help and new volunteers keep the rank full. In recent years new programs have begun in Jordan, China, and three countries of the former Soviet Union, Estonia Latvia, and Lithuania. Sixty four hundred volunteers now serve in 72 countries around the world. Of this group 61% are female, 92% are single and the median age is 25. The Peace Corps operates on an annual budget of $275 million dollars. We should all hope that it continues.

Chapter 5

Refugees and Landmines, Healing the Devastation of War

Chapter 3 discussed the activities of the United States Agency for International Development in their Humanitarian Assistance program. Those projects dealt with a variety of disasters, both natural and man-made. Of these it is the aftermath of war that leaves the cruelest human problems to be dealt with. At the beginning of the last century 90% of wartime casualties were soldiers. At the end of the century, 90% of wartime casualties are civilians and their injuries are not necessarily sustained during the period of conflict.

Any protracted fighting will set in motion floods of refugees, generally the children and others least able to care for themselves, with no particular destination except to escape the conflict. Once the fighting ends and the refugees return to their homes they may find their communities turned into killing fields because of buried anti-personnel landmines and unexploded munitions which can remain a concealed threat for years after the conflict ends.

The scale of these problems is enormous. A U.S. Department of State fact sheet states that in the year 2000, children in more than 50 countries were suffering from the effects of armed conflict. Of these more than 400,000 were unaccompanied refugees or internally displaced children and over 300,000 were child combatants. For each child who is killed or injured by physical violence, gunfire, or

41

landmines, many more are deprived of their basic physical, emotional, spiritual, and cultural needs. Millions of children have lost their parents, siblings, homes, and education. Girls especially are victimized in ways that can have a life-long impact.

The United States, in conjunction with other nations and international organizations, has several agencies that deal with the problems of children affected by war. USAID is one of these agencies and conducts a variety of programs that deal with different aspects of these problems.

- During conflict, or as soon as possible afterward these programs are designed to:

  Document, trace, and reunify children with families;

  Support psychosocial adjustment of children in distress;

  Facilitate reintegration of children into communities;

  Support formal and informal education opportunities;

- The Displaced Children and Orphans Fund has worked in 28 countries providing financial support to organizations that strengthen the capacity of families and communities to provide care. While this fund also provides resources for AIDS orphans, street children and disabled children, over half its budget assists children impacted by war

- The Patrick J. Leahy War Victims fund provides financial and technical assistance to improve the mobility and health of children and adult victims of war and to aid their reintegration into society.

The United States Department of State is also active in helping solve the problems of children and others who have suffered the impact of war through two of its own Bureaus.

- The Bureau of Population, Refugees and Migration contributes millions of dollars each year to activities that benefit refugee children, including those directly affected by armed conflict. These funds are contributed to support the worldwide activities of International Red Cross, the United Nations High Commissioner for Refugees, and other international agencies.

- The Bureau of International Organization Affairs provides funding for several United Nations Development Agencies including UNICEF. In past years the Bureau has been the largest single source of funds for UNICEF, funds provided for children at risk in a wide range of countries.

While the plight of the refugees is graphically illustrated by pictures of refugee camps in Africa, Asia and the Middle East on the evening television news, landmines offer no visible warning of their deadly presence. We see their presence only in pictures of people who have lost a foot, a leg, or a life from landmines that may have been planted years earlier.

The United States deals with the worldwide landmine problem through the State Departments Office of Humanitarian De-mining Programs. This is not a new venture. This effort started in 1988 when we came to the aid of war-torn Afghanistan, a nation faced with the enormous problem of seven million landmines planted in its soil. This has nothing to do with our current involvement in Afghanistan, it relates to an earlier cycle of warfare in that troubled country.

While the U.S. has not signed the International Land Mine Treaty it has, since 1988, provided assistance to forty nations who faced serious problems with landmines. That staggering number is a reminder of how violent and unstable parts of our world are. These are not our landmines. We did not plant them. We do, however, have the money, the equipment, and the personnel to help nations that suffer this blight.

The U.S. program is an interagency one that focuses the special skills of various elements of the Department of Defense, the U.S. Agency for International Development and the Department of State.

- The U.S. Special Forces of the Defense Department send teams to countries with landmine problems to train local personnel on mine awareness, mine detection, mapping and marking techniques, mine clearance and trauma care in the case of accidents involving mine-clearance personnel. The Special Forces bring specialized equipment with them on these training missions and leave it behind when the training is completed. The Department also funds research into new mine detection technologies.

- The Department of State assistance varies with the requirements of the mine-affected nation. It can provide equipment such as detectors, protection gear, explosives, foodstuffs, and ambulances. It can also provide office equipment and data base capabilities to coordinate mine removal activities. The Department also provides funds for both non-governmental and commercial de-mining operations.

The United States joins other countries and a variety of international organizations to support de-mining programs and it is possible to see results. In Cambodia, a country beset with severe landmine problems, by the year 2000 the casualty rate had declined by more than 90% since the end of hostilities. In February of that year the number of landmine casualties was 42, compared to 550 just three years earlier. Namibia and Rwanda in Africa are close to declaring themselves mine-free. So are the countries of Central America.

There is reason to hope that we may one day see the end of these problems - if we could somehow manage to permanently end the violence in those parts of the world that create the problems.

Direct Aid, Bring in the Experts

Chapter 6

The Volcano Disaster Assistance Program

Millions of people in the United States live their lives without a thought to the terrifying prospect of a volcanic eruption. Since most of the country shows no sign of ever having had any volcanic activity, there is no reason they should worry. The situation is entirely different on the Pacific Coast. California, Oregon. Washington, and Alaska are all located on the "Ring of Fire', the zone of volcanic activity that circles the Pacific Ocean. The state of Hawaii is an especially active volcano hot spot. All these share a history of recent volcanic activity and the likely prospect of having more.

Studying volcanoes and devising methods of anticipating if and when they will erupt is among the responsibilities of the United States Geological Survey, (the USGS). There is no current hope that we will ever be able to stop a volcano from erupting but understanding the warning signs they provide make it possible to take steps to minimize the loss of life and property. As a result the USGS has developed sensitive equipment to measure signs of early activity and the experience to interpret this data and can share this expertise with other countries.

In 1985 more than 23,000 people were killed in Armero, Colombia, and the city essentially wiped out, as a result of the eruption of the Nevado del Ruiz volcano. When the volcano first began to send out warning signs in 1984 no team of volcanologists existed that could rush to the scene and provide expert assistance. Since such a tragedy could occur in many other parts of the world, within a year the USGS and the U.S. Office of Foreign Disaster Assistance (part of the U.S. Agency for International Development) developed the Volcano Disaster Assistance Program, (VDAP), to respond to such volcanic crises wherever they occurred.

Working through USAID, and at the request of the host countries, VDAP can send an experienced team of USGS and other scientists to the volcanic site with a portable cache of state of the art monitoring equipment. It has proved to be effective in saving lives and property by determining the nature of the volcanic unrest and estimating the scale and time of the eruption for local authorities.

Volcanic eruptions are one of the Earth's most violent and dramatic agents of change. Powerful explosive eruptions can dramatically change the landscape for miles around the volcano itself, destroying homes, villages, roads, crop land and utilities. In a brief interval it can destroy a thriving community as it did in Armero, Columbia. Volcanologists who come to monitor the state of a volcano measure the changes caused by magma movement beneath the volcano which produces swarms of earthquakes, swelling or subsidence of a volcano's summit or flanks and the release of volcanic gases from the ground and vents. They establish measuring and recording equipment as close as possible to the active vents. Based on these observations and measurements they can make predictions about an eruption days or weeks in advance and take steps to minimize deaths and property damage.

VDAP is the only rapid-response volcano crisis team in the world. Its most notable success occurred during the catastrophic eruptions of Mount Pinatubo in the Phillipines in 1991. Working with local scientists of the Philippine Institute of Volcanology, the team brought in and set up a monitoring network to provide accurate readings on what was taking place underground. Based on the data provided by these instruments experts were able to predict that an extremely large and destructive eruption was about to take place.

The U.S. Geological Survey described it as "the largest volcanic eruption on Earth in more than 75 years. The most powerful phase of the eruption lasted more than ten hours, creating an enormous cloud of volcanic ash that rose as high as 22 miles into the air and grew to more than 300 miles across, turning day into night over central Luzon. Falling ash blanketed an area of thousands of square miles, and avalanches of hot ash (pyroclastic flows) roared down the slopes of the volcano and filled deep valleys with deposits of ash as much as 600 feet thick."

As a result of the forecast the evacuation area around the volcano was greatly enlarged. Movable equipment was removed from the area and one million residents were evacuated. While the damage to structures was great, there was little loss of life. The cost of the accurate scientific forecast of the size and scale this eruption, including salaries, helicopters, and other logistical support, was about $1.5 million dollars. Earlier work in the area and the cost of the USGS mobile monitoring capacity is estimated at $15 million dollars. Local authorities estimate that the successful forecasting prevented property losses of at least $250 million dollars. Far more important is the estimate that 5000 lives were saved.

Since that time VDAP has responded to 19 volcanic crises in Central and South America, the Caribbean, Africa, Asia, and the South Pacific. Each experience increases the knowledge that USGS scientists bring back to this country to apply to our own volcanic problems. At the same time it makes the response team increasingly valuable to developing countries that have no such skills themselves. VDAP clearly rates high as a gift from America.

As an added international service the U.S. Geological Survey teams with the Smithsonian Institute to publish a Weekly Volcanic Activity Report. A recent report listed ongoing activity in twelve volcanoes in eleven countries.

Chapter 7

The United States Forest Service Overseas

The United States Department of Agriculture is a complex and active organization that covers a surprising number of activities. One of these is the Forest Service, a complex organization in itself, which manages our National Forests.

In the course of administering the vast National Forests of the United States, the Forest Service has developed techniques and human skills that cannot easily be handed off to others. They have to be delivered in person. In responding to requests for assistance from other countries Forest Service International Programs can call on wildlife biologists, forest economists, hydrologists, disaster and fire management specialists, and policy makers from the Forest Service staff of thirty thousand people.

International Programs are normally conducted in partnership with the government involved, and other international aid agencies. The projects range from small to very large and vary widely from country to country. Protecting local water resources is a problem experienced in many countries and so is controlling wildfires. The two are closely related. Once the woodlands that protect the soil and slow down run-off are gone the soil is exposed to severe soil erosion and the streams to flooding. There are a variety of other problems the Forest Service International Programs can help with.

The following sample of projects that Forest Service International Programs is involved in is surprising because of the geographic spread of the sites where help is being offered and range of climatic conditions that are encountered there.

- In recent years China has experienced some of the most devastating floods in its history in large part due to over-cutting timber in the mountains where the major rivers originate. U.S. experts are now advising officials of the Chinese State Forestry Administration on reforestation programs to control the runoff and to restore the health of the woodlands. American foresters are helping to identify appropriate nursery stock for replanting areas that have been clear-cut and Forest Service entomologists are introducing programs for dealing with insect pests that are common to both Chinese and American Forests.

- The Rio Laja watershed in Mexico has deteriorated over time with increasing flooding, erosion and the loss of fertile farmland in the river bottom. Local groups wanted to deal with these problems but needed expert advice and funding which came from International Programs grants. As a result community activists have planted thousands of willows and cottonwoods and built hundreds of erosion control structures to stabilize the banks of the river and save their farmland.

- In the Middle East Forest Service experts confer with authorities in Israel, Jordan, and Turkey on watershed management as it applies to arid and semi-arid land. The problems of arid and semi-arid lands may seem an unlikely topic for the Forest Service to deal with but soil erosion is a serious problem in these areas and is one that the Service is familiar with.

- Following uncontrolled Indonesian wildfires in 1997 and 1998, that cast a smoke pall over much of Southeast Asia, Forest Service personnel joined a regional technical advisory committee to conduct an assessment of fire suppression capabilities in Brunei, Indonesia, Malaysia, Singapore and the Philippines.

- The Office of International Programs and Ducks Unlimited have recently announced a new partnership for the conservation and maintenance of priority wetlands for migratory birds and waterfowl. This expanded partnership with DU brings International Programs into a new international conservation role throughout the hemisphere.

- The forests of the Congo are the second largest intact tropical rainforest in the world and are an essential resource for the people in the area. The health of the forests is being threatened by deforestation and destructive logging practices. USDA Forest Service and the U.S. Agency for International Development are promoting the use of reduced-impact logging programs through careful location of logging roads, and skid trails. These improved practices will permit timber harvesting to continue without destroying the resource that is the economic foundation for the people in the area.

The work of the U.S. Forest Service International Program in Brazil is much larger in scale. Since 1991 the Forest Service has cooperated with the government of Brazil in addressing concerns about the problems facing that nations forests. The country is not only home to the world's largest rain forest and river, it has other areas, such as the Pantanal, that support a remarkable biodiversity. The health of Brazil's forests are important to the whole world.

Funded by the United States Agency for International Development the Forest Service lends scientific and technical expertise to Brazil. These experts work directly with their Brazilian counterparts. Because of its size and diversity the range of problems to be considered and dealt with in Brazil is especially diverse.

- Foreign insect pests are becoming increasingly destructive in Brazil's pine plantations. Tests are now being conducted on the use of parasitic wasps as a biological control.

- In the Amazon, the Forest Service links field research, training, and technical assistance on sustainable forestry practices specifically related to reduced impact timber harvesting,

- Maintaining conditions suitable for migratory birds and water fowl in the Pantanal, the worlds largest fresh-water ecosystem, is another long term concern.

- Fire is one of the most dangerous threats to the Amazon forest. The Forest Service provides technical assistance and training in fire prevention and suppression. It is also in a unique position to supply key research data and information to on forest fire dynamics and susceptibility.

At the other end of the scale in program size is one that is a favorite of mine.

Linda Torgerson, a civil engineering technician in the Tongass National Forest in Alaska, traveled halfway around the world to Madagascar to teach basic trail construction skills. For six weeks she taught two crews of conservation agents bridge planning, location, design, and construction in the trail systems being developed in their new national parks. The use of local hardwoods was stressed to keep the bridge structures in harmony with the local forest environments.

In human terms that is as direct and personal a gift of the knowledge, skill, and experience of American scientists and technicians helping other people help themselves as anyone could hope for.

Chapter 8

Power From the Sun for the Third World

When you examine the range of activities managed by the U.S. Department of Energy, it exhibits a split personality. It operates 25 Laboratories and Research Centers that study energy issues ranging from the most sophisticated studies of the heart of matter to simple renewable energy sources. It operates the Princeton Plasma Physics Laboratory at one end of the scale and the National Renewable Energy Laboratory at the other end.

The National Renewable Energy Laboratory focuses on improving the utilization of wind energy, solar energy, geothermal energy from the earth's interior and the conversion of farm products and agricultural waste to energy. It is naturally called the NREL. (Government writers seem to be unable to function without acronyms.)

While renewable energy technology is universally valuable, it is especially valuable in areas where no other energy options are available. As a consequence, NREL has a record of helping to bring electrical power to rural areas where it is completely lacking. Using its technology and experience it can plan systems that are appropriate for the locality and train staff to install and administer the operations.

A program carried out in West Bengal, India, illustrates how this approach works. India has more than 72,000 villages that are currently without electricity. Extending the power grid to all these sites would be extremely expensive and the low level of usage by the villagers would not justify the expense. In a joint 50-50 venture with the Government of India, NREL agreed to design systems appropriate for the area and train a local non-profit agency to install them.

Designs using photovoltaic units (solar panels) to provide electricity were developed for each village, depending on its special needs. A typical system might provide electricity for a village water pump, a vaccine refrigerator, a community street light, four hours of fluorescent lighting for the weaving center and home lighting systems with one nine watt fluorescent fixture and one thirty watt electrical outlet. A nine watt light would hardly be noticed in an American home and the electrical outlet seems limited but any light is better than no light and an electrical outlet that can power a radio or small TV can make a big difference in West Bengal.

Notice the priority given to providing power to the vaccine refrigerator. A reliable power source is an indispensable part of the local health system.

A local non-profit supplies information and advice, sells units to home owners and can provide maintenance and repair services. The intent of the project is not just to supply the equipment but to leave behind an organization that has the technical ability and experience to carry on the program. This system is in successful operation.

Projects that have been completed in Brazil show considerable variety in dealing with rural electrification. Some villages have photovoltaic systems similar to those used in West Bengal. In other areas that have been served by small local utilities, using diesel powered minigrids, hybrid systems have been designed. They employ photovoltaics, wind power, diesel and battery storage to lower operating costs and to increase the total power available to the grid. Using all of the renewable energy options in systems where they are most effective makes it possible to solve most rural electrification problem.

The National Renewable Energy Laboratory's Village Power program focuses on bringing in contributors and collaborators to make renewable energy systems available in parts of the world where no other source of power is available. In Uganda the Laboratory formed a partnership with the Hathaway Foundation, a non-profit organization, to provide power to village schools. When the children of the Wheelersburg Elementary School in Ohio and Stevenson Middle School in Los Angeles heard of the program they decided to share the money they had raised to bring solar power to their own schools, and joined the project. Various corporations provided solar panels, a satellite dish television, and computers. The US Agency for International Development financed the transport of the equipment and its installation and maintenance. Under this program the Hathaway foundation has installed over 400 solar electric systems in rural Uganda.

Over two billion people in developing countries, nearly one-third of the word's population, live without electrical service. As the examples discussed above show almost any reliable electric power can be helpful. Just having enough power to pump water, run a radio, or illuminate a workplace after dark, can be a real blessing.

Chapter 9

The Department of Justice Sends Help Overseas

In addition to its usual functions in law enforcement in this country and its joint activities with law enforcement agencies around the world the Department of Justice offers special assistance to foreign governments who need to improve their own policing systems. The International Criminal Investigative Training Assistance Program, or ICITAP, was created in 1986 in response to a request from the Department of State for assistance in training police forces in Latin America. The program, part of the Criminal Division of the Department, now sends assistance to countries around the world to help them develop law enforcement services based on democratic principles and respect for human rights.

ICITAP develops its training programs with the host governments to address their specific law enforcement problems. Programs are usually initiated by the Department of State, the National Security Council, and the host country. Funding for each program is provided by the State Department or the United States Agency for International Development.

Training is the basic focus of all the programs. It covers general and specialized courses for senior and supervisory officials, rank and file personnel and support staff. ICITAP also supports the development of police academies and the training of academy instructors so that police knowledge and skills can be kept up to date.

Technical Assistance provides short and long-term law enforcement specialists to study existing police systems and recommend new or reformed systems. The Forensics Program provides training and brings in up-to-date technology to improve crime scene investigations and develop appropriate laboratory procedures and policies.

In sending expert trainers and consultants on these overseas assignments ICITAP can draw on active and retired federal, state, and local criminal justice experts. These experts have been involved in Albania, Bosnia, Colombia, Croatia, East Timor, El Salvador, Georgia and Armenia, Ghana, Guatemala, Indonesia, Kosovo, Macedonia, Moldova, Nicaragua, Pakistan, and Senegal.

The best way to understand the kind of complex problems they must deal with is to look at some actual overseas programs. Albania, which experienced a general breakdown on public order in 1997, is a good example. Beginning in 1998 ICITAP provided strategic planners and management training to the leadership of the Albanian National Police to prepare a plan for developing a modern democratic police organization. In the next phase ICITAP began training Albanian Rapid Reaction Units directly to cope with civil disorder management in the northern region of the country bordering Kosovo and advisors were assigned to key police executives.

During the following phase Albania was so disrupted by a terrorist alert that training of Albanian police executives had to be shifted to the Polish National Police Academy. ICITAP could not return to Tirana, the Albanian capital, until the fighting in Kosovo ended.

In addition to training a national police force that could maintain order, special attention had to be given to controlling organized and transnational crime. Because of its location the country had a serious problem of illegal trafficking in drugs, weapons, and women and children. A Total Information Management System that connects the major ports and airports is being developed to combat smuggling activities. Together with this communication system eleven technical advisors are assigned to the Office of the Prime Minister, to the principal ports, to the Organized Crime Unit, and the Office of Professional Responsibility.

The ICITAP Program in East Timor is totally different. In contrast to Albania, where the problem was one of reorganizing and strengthening an existing police force to deal with both national and international crime, in East Timor the problem was to create a police force where none existed.

In 1999 hostilities between Indonesia and East Timor ended and a new country, (now called Timor Leste), emerged. The assignment for the U.S. State Department and ICITAP was to determine how best to assist the United Nations Transitional Administration for East Timor train 3000 new police officers to form an indigenous police force for the new country. As a result ICITAP took over training in supervision, management and administration, criminal investigations, and police academy development.

The ICITAP evaluation indicated that community-based policing skills were non-existent among the trainees and that they lacked the confidence and assertiveness to intervene in activities such as domestic violence without direct instructions by the trainers. Basic police skills were lacking not only in weapons handling and disturbance management but in such elementary skills as driving a vehicle. A lot of training was needed.

By the time the ICITAP program ends in 2004 the special courses provided will have developed supervisory and management skills, crime scene specialists, homicide investigators, and taught the principles of democratic policing.

The Office of Overseas Prosecutorial Development, Assistance, and Training

ICITAP has a sister organization that works in parallel with it called OPDAT. While ICITAP deals with training and development of police forces OPDAT does the same thing with the training of judges and prosecutors. OPDAT has a program in Albania facing the same problems as ICITAP. It is involved in such training programs in South and Central America, the Caribbean, Russia, the Newly Independent States of the Soviet Union and Central and Eastern Europe.

The Child Exploitation and Obscenity Section

The Criminal Division of the Department of Justice also operates the Child Exploitation and Obscenity Section (the CEOS). This section focuses on international training and policy development on child exploitation issues to eliminate the trafficking of women and children for sexual purposes. Because of the ease with which child pornography can be distributed via the Internet and the availability of inexpensive air travel sex tourism, particularly child sex tourism, has been growing.

CEOS attorneys conduct training sessions with prosecutors, police, government officials and non-governmental organizations, all of whom offer assistance to victims of this illegal trade in the developing democracies. The training focuses on legal reforms to ensure the protection of victims, development of multi-agency task forces to combat trafficking, and cooperation of law enforcement agencies with NGO's serving victims. Bulgaria, Macedonia, Romania, Latvia, Lithuania, Albania, Russia, Ukraine, Thailand, and El Salvador, have all received training from CEOS staff.

It is a violation of United States law for American citizens or permanent residents to go abroad for the purpose of having sex with children. As a result, CEOS not only helps other countries combat the illegal sex trade, it assists them in insuring that, if Americans are involved, they will be prosecuted.

Programs such as the three described in this chapter receive little public attention and it is doubtful that many Americans know about them. Yet it is clear that helping emerging democracies establish public order and combat crime is a gift of great value.

Chapter 10

The USAID and Higher Education

The United States Agency for International Development, as described in Chapter three, has six strategic goals in providing aid to the developing countries of the world.

1. Encourage economic growth and agricultural development;

2. Strengthen democracy and good government;

3. Build human capacity through education and training;

4. Stabilize world population and protect human health;

5. Protect the environment for long-term sustainability;

6. Promote humanitarian assistance.

An important activity in support of these goals is to use the talent and experience of American Colleges and Universities to help similar institutions in developing countries improve and expand their own capabilities to meet the needs of their countries. To achieve this collaboration USAID works with the Association Liaison Office for University Cooperation in Development, (ALO), which represents six leading associations of American public and private institutions of higher education.

USAID/Washington and its field missions throughout the world regularly seek educational institutions to support specific projects that are deemed important in the developing world. Bids are then invited on these projects. Unsolicited proposals that advance U.S. foreign assistance objectives are also accepted for review.

This is a program that has not received the public recognition it deserves. A look at the partnerships discussed below indicates what a strong system of higher education this country has and how much we can offer other countries. In the long term it is programs such as this that are the best hope of developing countries to cope with problems of poverty and poor health.

International Partnerships in Higher Education

This is one program that makes annual awards to Colleges and Universities. In the past five years 100 Partnership projects have been funded in 45 countries. The list is impressive, not only for its size but also for the range of activities covered as the selection below demonstrates.

- Indiana University is partnered with Moi University Faculty of Health Sciences in Kenya to more effectively manage HIV/AIDS in that country. Medical school education, health care delivery, and research have been improved and a new curriculum developed to train health-care workers in HIV risk reduction and counseling for testing and pre-natal HIV prophylaxis. A laboratory has been established for diagnosing sexually transmitted diseases and laboratory technicians are being trained for this work.

- The University of Wisconsin at Madison and the Universidad Nacional del Altiplano in Peru are working together to create a high-altitude-adapted milking cow for the impoverished altiplano region of Peru. The partners are currently developing in-vitro embryo production techniques that will permit them to cross-breed yaks (from high-altitude countries like Tibet) with local cows. Viable milk producing cows adapted to the high altitude regions of the Andes would be a boon for the region.

- The University of Texas at Austin and the Instituto Tecnologico y de Estudios Superiores de Monterrey, A.C. are working to provide judicial training and promote judicial professionalism at the state court level in Mexico. The partners will work with newly appointed judges to identify priority areas for judicial training and develop four pilot training programs in the areas of judicial professionalism and court management and administration.

But these examples hardly encompass the full range of partnership programs that are now in operation. Here are a few more of the 100 approved programs.

- Purdue University is retraining faculty and training workers in agriculture in the war torn country of Afghanistan.

71

- Georgia State University is teaching women to manage small business in the Central Asian country of Georgia.

- The University of Delaware is enhancing teaching skills of science and math teachers in Peru.

- The University of Delaware is training public officials in coastal management in Jamaica.

- Cleveland State University is establishing training programs to help small manufacturing firms improve productivity and quality in Zambia.

- Tiffin University will assist in creating a School of Criminal Justice in Romania.

Special Initiative Programs

These are sponsored by USAID offices in various countries to deal with special local needs.

- The Special Initiative in Egypt was awarded to Georgia State University to support a partnership with the Alexandria Institute of Technology to develop Egypt's human resource capacity in business management with a focus on international marketing.

- The Special Initiative in Macedonia was awarded to an Indiana University led consortium to support the development of a new multi-lingual, multi-cultural university in Tetovo, a predominantly Albanian community in northwest Macedonia

- The Special Initiative in El Salvador supports the partnership between the Metropolitan Community College in Omaha and the Universidad Centroamericana to support a country-wide program in early childhood education, targeting children up to six years old from poor rural families

The Workforce Training Partnership Program

This is conducted with the American Association of Community Colleges, supports the creation of partnerships to improve the ability of developing countries to train skilled workers for the workforce.

- The Russia Nursing Development Project teams the Harford Community College of Maryland with the Moscow Medical College #1 to improve the training of nurses in Russia. Nurses in that country were being trained to perform only the most basic skills, seriously limiting the assistance they could provide their patients. The Development Project will expand the training and role of nurses to promote a more efficient use of health care resources. The partners conduct workshops to improve the teaching skills of the Moscow Medical College #1 Faculty They will also develop clinical instruction materials and are revising the curriculum, using the nursing program at Harford

Community College as a model. New course materials will also be distributed to other Russian medical schools.

- The Tanzania Information Technology Partnership teams Columbus State Community College with the Dar Es Salaam Institute of Technology and Vicatel, a local business, to provide training in information technology to Tanzanians in both the public and private sectors. These participants will initially train Tanzanians who will serve as teachers and go on to create a self-sustaining Information Technology Institute in Dar Es Salaam with the capacity to train 200 students per year.

    The Tanzanian participants began their studies using an online course offered by Columbus State Community College. During the next phase faculty from CSCC will travel to Tanzania to co-teach this new curriculum, to establish the Information Technology Institute and to select the first group of trainees.

- The St. Louis Community College teamed with the Guyana Ministry of Education to develop a two-year curriculum to train certified land surveyors in post secondary institutes in Guyana. A first-year class of 20 students enrolled in the course. The partners continue to work to expand the training, increase the rate of delineation of agricultural lands, to encourage private ownership, and ultimately to increase agricultural production.

- San Diego Community College District and Centros de Capacitacion Tecnologica Industrial have collaborated on a partnership to support regional economic development by improving the employability of the Mexican workforce through education and training. The partners worked with business and industry to develop model curricula and instructional materials for certification programs in electronics and welding particularly for those employed in the export industries where international standards must be met.

This is only a sample of the variety and scope of USAID's involvement with American Universities and Colleges in delivering assistance to developing countries.

Sharing Technology

Chapter 11

The Global Positioning System, a Personal Navigator

The Global Positioning System is a perfect example of the gifts that this country has given to the world. It was developed, financed, and is operated by the United States. While it was originally conceived for military purposes the benefits are now freely available to all who want to use them. It solves the age-old problem of finding out exactly where you are in the world and works equally well for someone cruising in dangerous waters or trying to locate a street address in a strange city.

Through the ages one of humankind's most difficult problems has been finding its way around on the globe we inhabit. Navigating in your own neighborhood isn't hard but finding your way in the vast plains and deserts of the earth is not easy. Even more difficult, and perilous, is the problem of navigating across the trackless seas.

Early merchant traders and seafarers learned that the stars could be used to give a sense of direction, when they could be seen, and later learned that naturally magnetized minerals could be used as a primitive compass to point the way North. Eventually, the creation of more accurate and portable instruments made it possible to determine latitude, one's north-south position between the equator and the poles. That was a real accomplishment. Yet, since both Cairo and New Orleans, and an infinite number of other places, are on the same latitude, it hardly solved the location problem.

What remained was the problem of determining longitude, the east-west position around the circumference of the earth. It took a long time. It could be done by setting up an astronomical observatory at any given spot on earth but this hardly served global travelers. As international traffic increased, and the reach of the European nations grew to encircle the globe, the toll of ships lost due to navigation failures grew.

These losses finally became so pressing that the government of Great Britain established a cash prize for a reliable means of establishing longitude that could be used on ships at sea. There were several elements in the final solution but the key element was not a better understanding of astronomy or improved instruments for taking star sights, but through the development of a more accurate time piece than had ever before been achieved. By producing a portable clock that faithfully retained the current time at the Royal Naval Observatory in Greenwich, just down the River Thames from London, wayfarers and seafarers could locate themselves with reasonable accuracy anywhere on the globe.

It took centuries for the art of navigation to arrive at the point where both latitude and longitude could be easily established with portable equipment and it was a real triumph of human ingenuity. Today, this old technology has been largely replaced by satellites and atomic clocks in a new technology called the Global Positioning System.

The Global Positioning System was conceived thirty five years ago as a result of the military's need for a quick and highly accurate system for establishing location. Its principal element is a fleet of 24 satellites, each equipped with four atomic clocks, that circle the globe on a precise schedule. The system is managed and operated by five monitor stations located around the globe and a master control station in Colorado.

The GPS is not just high technology, it is the result of the convergence of two streams of technical development that have met in a wonderfully useful form. It started with the development of rocket propulsion systems capable of positioning large satellites in space and maintaining them in precise locations. A parallel stream of technical progress was taking place in the area of time-keeping. In the 1930's Physicist I.I. Rabi, then at Columbia University was "able to tune microwaves to the frequency of atoms, thus enabling the design of atomic clocks". Other researchers improved on this foundation, collecting Nobel Prizes along the way, until the 1950's when the United States built NIST-7, the most accurate clock in the world. The term "accurate" used in this context goes far beyond anything we know in the normal world. Sporting events can be measured in thousandths of a second by normal means. Atomic clocks measure time in billionths of a second. That is important. An error as small as one billionth of a second could produce an error of one foot in ground location.

Though the benefits of the Global Positioning System to people everywhere were obvious from the beginning of the project it was reserved exclusively for military use until 1983 when Korean Airlines flight 007 wandered over Russian territory and was shot down by a Russian jet. At that point President Reagan ordered the Department of Defense to modify the system so that the highest and most accurate level of service could be reserved for military use and a less accurate service could be made available for civilian use.

Since this change in policy use of the system has grown at an explosive rate. Simple hand held GPS receivers can be bought for less than $200. Automobiles can be equipped with systems that not only show where you are but will also track your location as you move through the city streets. Systems are available for marine and aircraft use. A wristwatch GPS receiver is available for the ultimate in personal convenience.

The system is excellent for finding things. If you need to know where your delivery trucks or your police cars are located at any moment a GPS unit on the vehicle will report its location so the dispatcher can spot it on the map. Wildlife biologists can track the species they are studying and chart its movements. Locating a specific shipping container in those big seaport storage yards is no problem with GPS locators.

When the tunnel under the English Channel was dug, GPS receivers were used to ensure that excavators working from each side of the Channel would meet in the proper alignment. We are far from knowing all the ways the system can be put to beneficial use.

The Global Positioning System was developed, installed, and is operated by the Department of Defense for the United States

Government and offered to rest of the world for anyone who wants to use it, free of charge, a most valuable and useful gift from America.

Chapter 12

The Internet

Thirty three years ago the first "internet" was formed when the Department of Defense's Advanced Research Project Agency, DARPA, connected several existing computer networks into ARPANET. It was originally conceived both as a high-speed system to permit scientists to share data and access remote computers at research centers in the United States and for military command and control purposes in case of war. In 1969 researchers at Stanford Research Institute, the University of California at Los Angeles, the University of California at Santa Barbara and the University of Utah connected to form the first hosts of ARPANET.

Over the next decade as the demands on the system grew the National Science Foundation became increasingly involved and, by the mid 1980's assumed the primary financial support. The increased demand for advanced networking and research computing capabilities led the NSF to invest 200 million dollars in the development of the high-speed backbone called NSFNET. In 1995 with the private commercial market thriving, the National Science Foundation decommissioned the NSFNET and the explosive growth of the Internet took off.

Since then, it has developed into an international network covering the globe. The world has known other communication achievements such as radio, the telegraph, and the telephone but none of these spread around the globe with the speed of the Internet.

Today it provides nearly instantaneous interchange of data, information, sound, visuals, news, and gossip. Internet connections are a routine necessity in business operations, can be found in tens of thousands of schoolrooms and libraries, and provide the economic life-blood for the countless Internet coffeehouses and cafes that sell access to the net. This growth has been accelerated because of technical contributions made by many individuals, both in this country and abroad. Still, the system itself, nurtured and funded by the United States, has become a gift to the world.

To make the original DARPA concept work required not just one technical breakthrough, but a series. Fundamental to the process was the development of packet switching. It is easy for most people to understand that the telephone conversation they carry on with someone on the other edge of the continent is possible because there is a continuous connection between the two phones. The Internet works on an entirely different basis. It breaks messages into packets which are then forwarded individually by routers through any open connections available. These are then reassembled at the destination into a coherent transmission. When you consider that millions of messages and billions of packets are in the system at any time, this seems like a recipe for chaos but it works. Lay persons should be glad that there are people who can work these things out so we don't have to.

Early in its development, when still known as ARPANET, and still intended to be used only for research purposes, it became clear that exchanging messages between individuals would be an important addition to the system. Researchers also need to talk to each other. Ultimately, as the net migrated from a focus on defense needs to an all-purpose public system, message exchange via Email became its heaviest use.

While Email remains the most common use for individuals, it is not the only one. They can also check their bank account online, make airline and hotel reservations, make almost any kind of purchase, download music, play the stock market, research a paper, and inevitably spend hours chatting or arguing with complete strangers. For an individual, an internet connection is a one wire connection to the world.

Perhaps more important, though not so obvious, is the impact of the Internet on commerce and economics. Any company that makes or sells merchandise normally bought by individuals will surely have a web site that displays their merchandise, provides specifications, prices, and accepts orders. A different form of net trade is between giant corporations and their suppliers of goods and services. By posting requests for bid proposals on their web site, a manufacturer is in immediate contact with all their suppliers so that routine procurement is simplified.

Any report on the Internet is bound to be an interim report. Where it may go next and what it may become are unknown. If it never changes, however, its benefits are obvious. What started life as a Defense Department project to expedite scientific research has become an international system for exchanging information. It marks a profound change in the way the world communicates and the way the world works.

Chapter 13

The National Oceanic and Atmospheric Administration

The National Oceanic and Atmospheric Administration (NOAA), is not a name that many people in this country recognize yet it has as much to do with our daily lives as any agency of the United States Government. Every day it delivers the weather reports. Will it rain? Snow? Will swells coming in from a far away storm bring good surfing? Will Hurricane Henry actually hit the South Carolina coast or will it move harmlessly out to sea? Or will it change its mind and give North Carolina a sledgehammer blow?

Collecting and distributing this information is not only important to us, it is equally important to our neighbors and it wouldn't be easy for them to get. That's why NOAA is included here. It freely broadcasts essential storm and weather data to anyone who can use it, here or abroad. NOAA is a great giver of gifts.

NOAA is part of the Department of Commerce. While its current name is rather new, it includes components that date from the early days of this country. The U.S. Coast Guard was one. The National Marine Fisheries Service is another. Its overall assignment is to cover the fields of Oceanic and Atmospheric Science. It has an extensive program of laboratory research in these sciences. It operates the National Climatic Data Center in Asheville, North Carolina, the worlds largest active archive of weather data and, as you might expect, responds to requests for data from all over the world.

In 1960 NOAA began to launch satellites in polar orbit to provide a picture of how the weather was evolving over broad stretches of the globe. In 1966, as rocket propulsion powerful enough to lift large satellites into geostationary orbit became available, it launched the first of the geostationary satellites. They reside at an elevation of 22,300 miles above the equator and remain fixed over one spot on the earth's surface. Unlike Polar-orbiting Operational Environmental Satellites (POES), the Geostationary Operational Environmental Satellites, (GOES), can provide continuous monitoring of the earth's atmosphere and surface over a large region of the Western Hemisphere.

Fortunately we don't need to understand the extremely complicated technology that makes these satellites work. All we care about is that we get the critical information about weather that we need.

The best way to understand how this data benefits us is to look at the operations of NOAA's National Hurricane Center in Miami, Florida. The Center maintains a continuous watch on tropical cyclones over the Atlantic, Caribbean, and Gulf of Mexico from June 1 through November 30. The Eastern Pacific hurricane season runs from May 15 through November30. It prepares and distributes hurricane watches and warnings for the general public and marine and military advisories in both the domestic and international communities.

As GOES satellites pick up the first indications of a hurricane forming the information is broadcast to the public for the benefit of Americans and our neighbors in other countries. As hurricanes move in from the Atlantic, long before they pose a direct danger to the United States, the countries and island nations of the Gulf of Mexico and the Caribbean need this early warning to minimize the loss of life and destruction of property that normally result from these powerful storms.

Americans are accustomed to seeing Hurricane Center personnel reporting on the progress, wind power, and probable landfall of the newest threat on television. These are followed with intense interest in Florida, along the Gulf coast, and the Atlantic Seaboard. Defensive measures are planned and shifted as new data indicates that the storm path is changing. Television viewers in this country are familiar with pictures of long lines of automobiles moving inland from the coast to find safer ground.

Hurricanes have a distinctive form. They are a violent mass of moisture laden, wind-driven air, moving out of tropical waters, and circling an open center that is relatively calm. The data about these storms provided by satellites is supplemented by reports from Hurricane Center airplanes that follow the storms and, against all logic, fly through the extreme turbulence of the storm itself into the "eye" around which the storm mass circles. During their passage through the storm and into the eye the planes collect and transmit meteorological data. They also collect location data by dropping Global Positioning System receivers.

Predicting where a hurricane will make its landfall on our Gulf and Atlantic coasts is a matter followed with intense interest in those states likely to be affected. It is easy to lose sight of the fact that it may make a number of landfalls among the islands and island nations of the Caribbean and the information is equally important to them. The Hurricane Center in Miami has lots of friends along the hurricane path.

Weather activities in Miami don't stop with the end of the hurricane season. During the "off-season" the Hurricane Center provides training for U.S. emergency managers and representative from many other countries that are affected by tropical cyclones. The Tropical Analysis and Forecast Branch provides year-round weather information including satellite interpretation and satellite rainfall estimates for the international community.

Severe storms also occur along the Pacific Coast and NOAA's GOES satellites provide critical information to Mexico and the Central American Countries where they strike most often. Weather forecasters dealing with major storms share one frustration with volcanologists. They may be able to forecast where and when the disaster will strike so that people can take steps to protect their property and flee to safer ground, but nothing on earth can stop or turn aside these natural forces.

The COSPAS-SARSAT System

The term "COSPAS-SARSAT" wouldn't mean anything to most people, but if you were in a fishing boat, sinking off the coast of

Alaska, it could mean the difference between life and death. This strangely named system represents one of those international endeavors that are such a pleasure to report because they show how effective nations can be when they cooperate to make the seas safer for vessels of all countries.

SARSAT began in 1970 when a plane carrying two U.S. Congressmen crashed in a remote region of Alaska. In spite of a massive search, no trace of them has ever been found. In response to this tragedy, Congress mandated that all aircraft in the United States carry an Emergency Locator Transmitter designed to automatically activate after a crash and transmit a homing signal.

After several years of reliance on the ELT system a satellite based system, SARSAT, was developed in a joint effort by the United States, Canada, and France. A similar system, COSPAS, was developed by Russia. In 1979 these countries joined their efforts and by 1984 their satellite system was declared fully operational. Since then 25 other nations have joined the original founders to operate 28 ground stations and 15 mission control systems.

NOAA plays an important role in COSPAS-SARSAT. Its Geostationary satellites can instantly detect emergency signals, and relay them to the U.S. Mission Control center which automatically sends them on to rescue forces around the world. One of the principal rescue forces is the United States Coast Guard. More than 12,000 lives have been saved since the system began to operate in 1982.

The "El Nino" Story

In addition to reporting the daily variations of weather that affect our lives so much, NOAA is engaged in long range weather research that identifies weather cycles that have extremely important consequences around the globe. One of these is the El Nino cycle. What follows is a simple explanation of a complicated phenomenon.

In normal, i.e. non-El Nino, conditions, the trade winds blow from east to west across the tropical Pacific. These winds pile up warm surface water in the western Pacific so that the sea surface is about 18 inches higher in Indonesia than it is along the coast of South America and about 14 degrees warmer. This has two beneficial effects. As the surface water off the east coast of South America is moved to the west, nutrient rich colder water wells up from the ocean depths and fishing is good. Conditions are also good at the other end of the system. Rainfall is found in rising air over warm water so Indonesia gets adequate rainfall.

The El Nino label applies to the situation that occurs when this favorable condition is reversed. Warm water is not moved away from the coast of South America so there is no upwelling of nutrient rich cold water and fishing declines. In addition, rainfall follows the warm water eastward and unusually heavy rainfall and flooding can occur along the west coast of the Americas. The decrease in water temperature in the western Pacific reduces rainfall and may create severe drought conditions in Australia and Indonesia.

The affects of an El Nino condition are obviously highly important to many countries. To provide continuing data NOAA has established an array of 72 moored buoys in the Equatorial Pacific Ocean that measure temperature, currents, wind speed and chemical concentrations in the water. This data is transmitted daily to researchers and forecaster around the world in real time.

The programs described here do not provide an exhaustive catalogue of NOAA activities and contributions. They should be enough, however, to make it clear that NOAA offers the world some valuable Gifts from America.

Medicine and Public Health

Chapter 14
Some Star Medical Performers

Not all publicly supported medical research in this country originates at the National Institutes of Health or the Centers for Disease Control. Nor is it necessarily anonymous. When a research team led by a dynamic individual produces a cure for a disease that is widely feared as a killer, you can expect that leader to become a medical hero. That is what happened to Major Walter Reed, who lead the team that solved the problem of yellow fever, and to Dr Jonas Salk and Dr Albert Sabin who each developed a successful vaccine for polio.

An Army Officer Wins the Battle Against Yellow Fever

The last part of the nineteenth century saw a great breakthrough in medical understanding. Due to the pioneering work of such scientists as Louis Pasteur and Robert Koch in Europe, the germ theory of infectious disease opened the field of bacteriology. Walter Reed was a young officer in the United States Army Medical Corps who had served in many frontier posts but retained a fascination with research. An appointment in Baltimore gave him an opportunity to enroll at Johns Hopkins University as a student of bacteriology and pathology. This work prepared him for his later assignment to determine the cause of yellow fever and find the way to control it.

Yellow fever was a constant problem in the tropics and swept the eastern United States in a series of epidemics between 1596 and 1900. Not always fatal, the death rate was still alarming, varying from a normal rate of forty percent to as high as eighty-five percent. During the Spanish-American War, more men died of yellow fever than were killed by enemy action. That war had just ended when Reed was assigned to lead a team to investigate the disease and find a means of controlling it.

Medical experimentation in those days took a lot of courage. At the Columbia Barracks, outside of Havana, the team set up a series of screened rooms where volunteers were subjected to various infectious agents to see what happened. One by one they were eliminated until the culprit was found. Yellow fever, the feared "Yellow Jack," was carried by the Anopheles mosquito. Some volunteers died in order to gain that knowledge. In 1929 Congress awarded a special gold medal to the twenty-four brave men who participated in these experiments.

The mosquitoes breed in still fresh water whether in swampy ground, cisterns, or discarded tin cans. By eliminating those conditions near human habitations the mosquitoes, and Yellow Fever, could be eliminated.

The work of Walter Reed and his team had immediate practical results. French efforts to build a canal in Panama had been frustrated by the high death rate from yellow fever. By rigorously eliminating places where mosquitoes could breed, outbreaks of the fever were controlled in the Canal Zone and the American builders, who took over the canal construction once the French had left, were able to complete the work.

The United States did not have many medical heroes at that time so Major Reed was honored both in medical circles and by the public. The lasting testimonial to his accomplishments is the Walter Reed Army Medical Center in Washington D.C.

Polio, the Curse of Summer

In the middle of the last century one of the greatest threats to the peace of mind of American parents was the prospect that their children might be stricken by polio myelitis, the dread infantile paralysis. The fact that small children seemed to be the favorite target was one terrifying factor. The other was the image of small children existing in "iron lungs," medical devices that controlled the breathing for the most seriously affected victims, or spending their lives walking with heavy leg braces and a cane. In 1952, at the peak of the epidemic, a total of 57,000 cases were recorded in the United States.

Summer was the time of highest concern. Parents were advised to keep their children away from parties, movies, swimming pools, and any other gathering places. This made summer vacation hard for children and explained the urge to get the children out of town to any place where the danger was less.

One frightening aspect of polio is that it could remain latent for long periods of time and suddenly return. This can happen even if the infection is so mild that it is not identified as polio. We successfully raised three daughters through the polio epidemic under the ceaseless supervision of my wife and felt that we had scored a victory.

Given the level of concern about polio, it is not hard to understand the universal joy that parents felt when the first successful polio vaccine was introduced in 1952.

The Salk Vaccine

Since polio was such a concern of the American people many researchers raced to find a vaccine to prevent it. Dr. Jonas Salk won that race.

A graduate of New York University's medical school, he focused his career on medical research. Originally he worked on developing a successful influenza vaccine. Later he was invited to continue his work at the University of Pittsburgh where he began work on a polio vaccine. Using techniques pioneered by others, he found that a killed virus injected into a child could produce a response in the immune system. In other words, it acted as a successful vaccine. In 1952 he inoculated the first volunteers, including himself, his wife, and their three sons in a demonstration that proved it was both safe and effective. This was shortly followed by a mass inoculation of over one million children.

Salk's work was supported by the Infantile Paralysis Foundation whose "March of Dimes", fund raising drives were extremely effective in raising money to combat polio. By the middle fifties, polio was no longer the terrifying specter in this country that it had been. Salk was a national hero.

The Sabin Vaccine

Dr. Albert Sabin was also a graduate of New York University. He subsequently worked in polio research at the Rockefeller Institute for Medical Research. Following service in the Army Medical Corps, he returned to his research at the University of Cincinnati College of Medicine and Children's Hospital Research Foundation.

Sabin's approach to the creation of a vaccine was radically different from Salk's.

The Salk vaccine used a virus that had been killed by treatment with formaldehyde but still retained the ability to stimulate the body's immune reaction. The Salk vaccine had to be injected. Sabin's vaccine used a live virus that had been weakened, so that it still stimulated an immune reaction but was not dangerous. The Sabin vaccine could be taken orally and in time this became the favored form of vaccination

While both men were honored for their achievements in countries around the world there was considerable dissension within the medical community about the merits of the Salk approach and the fact that no credit was given for earlier research work that paved the way for his vaccine. It does seem strange that the only Nobel Prize for work on polio was given to Dr John Enders of Harvard who did the essential preliminary work that all researchers used.

The polio story may seem terribly out of date to people living in this country. Can we really call the Salk and Sabin vaccines gifts from America? The answer to that is emphatically yes! Worldwide, there were approximately 350,000 new polio cases each year during the 1980's. By the year 2000 the number had dropped to 2400 new cases per year. Those vaccines have been a blessing for parents and children all over the world.

For the parents in this country who still remember the terror of facing each summer with small children to protect, Salk and Sabin, either one or both, are heroes we won't forget.

Chapter 15

The National Institutes of Health

The National Institutes of Health, part of the U.S. Department of Health and Human Services, is an international powerhouse in uncovering new knowledge that leads to better health for everyone. With an annual budget exceeding 24 billion dollars it conducts research in its own laboratories, supports the research of other scientists both here and in other countries, helps train research investigators, and supports the dissemination of medical information. About ten percent of the budget supports work done by the NIH in its own labs. Eighty two percent is spent on grants and contracts supporting research and training in more than 2000 research institutions in the U.S. and other countries. At any given time the NIH supports as many as 35,000 grants. This is a massive research program. Given this level of activity, plus the work being done by similar institutions in other countries, it is puzzling that the world still has so many health problems.

The NIH operates from a 300 acre campus in Bethesda, Maryland. The 14 story clinical center admits 7000 inpatients each year, some of them coming from around the world to participate in clinical studies. Another 68,000 patients participate as outpatients.

The Institute also operates off-campus sites for Environmental Health Sciences, the Gerontology Research Center, the Animal

Center, the Addiction Research Center, and the Rocky Mountain Laboratories for Allergy and Infectious Diseases.

The National Library of Medicine is a center for medical information, publishing the Index Medicus, a comprehensive monthly listing of articles appearing in the worlds leading medical journals. A computerized version of the Index is known as MEDLINE.

Since the work done at the Institutes deals with the health problems of the human race it can all be regarded as a gift from America. They have the accomplishments to make this claim. The problem comes in sorting through the vast array of work they have undertaken over the past one hundred years to select a few representative examples of their achievements. The nature of the work they do tends to obscure these accomplishments since they focus on new knowledge concerning the nature of disease rather than the ultimate treatment. If the world ever sees a pill that will immediately cure the common cold it will probably not come from the NIH, but the original research that makes this breakthrough possible probably will.

The Fruits of Medical Research

Reading through endless pages of NIH research summaries quickly reveals how hard it is to distinguish in advance what will prove to be an important breakthrough. Here are two sequential entries:

- "a single gene was found to make laboratory mice more friendly and affectionate toward their cage mates."

- "created transgenic mice that showed enhanced performance in six different memory tests."

The NIH isn't really interested in breeding more affectionate mice or improving their memory. Those reports are from studies that trace the influence of genes on behavior, a topic that could be important to all of us.

Another entry seemed, at least to this reader, to make a true breakthrough in understanding the human mind. "By repeatedly scanning the brains of children 3 to 15 years old over a four year period scientists were able to see (that) between six and thirteen the highest growth rates were in the region specialized for language. Somewhere between the ages of eleven and fifteen growth in this region slows down, reflecting the difficulty most people have in learning new languages after the age of 12."

Rather than choose between such entries, the following examples were taken from the NIH "Series of Discoveries" papers.

Preventing Severe Diarrheal Disease in Infants

While the battle with AIDS dominates the current news, an equally tragic and much longer running battle against rotavirus has finally been won. The rotavirus is hardly a household word but it is the single biggest cause of life-threatening diarrhea in children under

2, affecting approximately 130 million infants and children worldwide. An estimated 2000 children die each day from rotavirus.

The attack on this devastating killer illustrates how basic research conducted by the NIH leads to treatments. In this case, once the rotavirus had been identified as the killer, its structure was studied to determine what elements were responsible for triggering an immune response from the body. With this knowledge researchers were able to produce an effective vaccine.

However the job was still not done. An agreement was reached with Wyeth-Ayerst Laboratories to carry on with the development, testing, and marketing of the vaccine, activities that the National Institutes of Health do not undertake.

Work has not stopped with the development and distribution of the vaccine. Efforts continue to both improve its effectiveness and reduce the cost. This vaccine is a gift of great value to the children of the world.

A Typhoid Vaccine for Small Children

A recent development is the first vaccine capable of protecting children ages 2 to 5 against typhoid fever. It is not only very effective, it is virtually free of side effects. Spread by fecal contamination of drinking water or food or by person to person contact, typhoid fever is a common disease in countries without adequate sanitation systems.

Currently about 16 million people worldwide develop typhoid each year and 600,000 die from it.

Improving Transplant Success

When the surgical transplantation of human organs was first undertaken, a fundamental problem was the tendency of the body's immune system to identify the transplant as a foreign invader and to reject it. NIH supported research led to the discovery of cyclosporine, a drug that suppressed the immune system and increased the chances of a successful transplant. Today, tens of thousands of transplants are performed around the world each year and thousands more critically ill patients await the availability of organs for transplanting.

Unfortunately, drugs like cyclosporine are highly toxic and require a lifelong regime to effectively suppress the immune system. This leaves the patient open to other infections the immune system would normally deal with.

In the past ten years NIH supported scientists have made new findings about the immune response that is leading to a different approach to transplant rejection. Rather than turning off the entire immune system, this new approach seeks to turn off only the specific immune cells that attack the transplant. People all around the world hoping for a trouble-free transplant may find the answer in this new therapy. Even more, it may open the way to new treatments for other immunologic disorders.

Preventing the Transfer of the HIV Virus from Mother to Infant

One of the saddest aspects of the AIDS tragedy is that the HIV virus that precedes AIDS is so frequently transmitted from mother to child. A single oral dose of Nevirapine given to an HIV infected

109

woman in labor and another to her baby within three days of birth can reduce the transmission of the virus by half. Used consistently in developing countries this treatment could save from 300,000 to 400,000 children from developing AIDS each year.

A Breakthrough in the Battle with Ebola Virus

As you will see in the chapter about the Centers for Disease Control, the Ebola Virus is a super killer for which no cure is yet known. Some strains of the virus kill 90% of the people it infects. Research supported by the NIH has identified the protein in the virus that causes the massive internal bleeding that kills people. That in itself is not a cure, but it illustrates the step by step process by which medical research makes progress. Researchers can now focus on new drugs or vaccines to combat the deadly effect of the virus.

It would be possible to expand this list greatly but it wouldn't serve the purpose of this book. The point is that the National Institutes of Health carry on a massive program to find the means to protect human health. In doing this they support research efforts in laboratories in other countries as well as our own. The work of the NIH is not only a blessing for Americans, it is a blessing for people everywhere.

Chapter 16

The Centers for Disease Control

The United States has an exceptionally strong lineup in the ongoing battles with disease and ill health. The National Institutes of Health conducts fundamental research into the nature of disease. The Centers for Disease Control and Prevention, also an agency of the Department of Health and Human Services, has a more proactive role. Its mission is to "promote health and quality of life by preventing and controlling disease, injury, and disability." CDC has a broad mandate with personnel assigned to 45 countries around the world.

The CDC operates as a series of Centers dealing with major health issues such as Birth Defects, Chronic Disease, Environmental Health, Infectious Disease, HIV, STD, and TB Prevention and others equally important. Because medical problems have no sense of borders, or national origin, the Centers are involved in these problems around the globe. Much that we learn in dealing with local problems applies to people in other countries as well and the reverse is equally true. This is a good place to note that the process works two ways. Other countries have medical research establishments and CDC works with them frequently, sharing information, equipment and specialized lab space.

Since the focus of this book is on things that our government and other agencies in this country do that is beneficial to people in other countries as well as our own a good place to look is the CDC's

Center for Infectious Diseases and its battles with outbreaks of mysterious diseases at home and abroad. A historic example would be the campaign to solve the puzzle of Legionnaire's Disease in the United States. Another would be a devastating epidemic of viral hemorrhagic fever in Africa labeled Ebola Fever.

The full story of these two campaigns, and a number of others, is reported in Gerald Astor's book, "The Disease Detectives. It is recommended reading for anyone who wants to understand the complex methods used to identify a previously unknown disease and the development of a campaign to control it.

Legionnaire's Disease

In 1976 the American Legion held their convention at the Bellevue Stratford Hotel in Philadelphia. While the activities at the convention were routine, the aftermath was deadly. As the Legionnaires dispersed to their homes strange medical reports began to come into public health authorities in Pennsylvania. Doctors were attempting to treat extremely ill patients without having any idea what the illness was—and finding that nothing worked. Sensing an emergency beyond their experience the Pennsylvania health authorities called the Centers for Disease Control.

While the list of cases clearly centered on Legionnaires and the Bellevue Stratford Hotel, there were strange inconsistencies. Thirty eight of the victims had been near the hotel but had never been in it. Even more surprising, none of the hotel staff came down with the disease. The media, appropriately, gave the outbreak a lot of coverage and there was much public apprehension.

Finding the infectious agent and the source of the infection proved extremely difficult. One thing that became clear with the passage of time was that you did not get the disease from someone who had it. You had to be infected directly by the mysterious agent. It took long and tedious work in the lab to finally identify the infectious agent, ultimately labeled "legionella". That helped but did nothing to answer the question of how it infected the Legionaires.

It took a lot more detective work to demonstrate that the cooling tower in the hotels air conditioning system provided the breeding ground for legionella. Its normal operation spread infection throughout the hotel. When it overflowed, as it did occasionally, it spread a fine mist of legionella on the streets around the hotel, infecting passersby. How did the staff escape? They didn't. The legionella condition in the cooling tower had existed for a long time. Once the researchers knew what to look for in the staff blood tests, they found antibodies indicating an earlier, mild, infection that gave staff members immunity when the devastating outbreak occurred.

This is the kind of detective work the Center for Disease Control does well. The payoff for the time and intense effort expended on this case is that it solved a lot of other mysterious cases, here and abroad that had never been resolved. Legionella had been hiding in air conditioning systems, shower heads, and other permanent water sources for a long time both in the United States and other countries. A welcome victory for us and every country where legionella may be hiding.

While the Legionaires Disease case shows the National Center for Infectious Disease operating at home, it also responds to outbreaks of infectious disease in other parts of the world. The rationale for this is clear. No lethal infectious disease is more than a plane ride from the United States. We have recently seen an outbreak of West Nile Fever in the U.S. It isn't clear how it arrived. It could have walked off an airplane when passengers from overseas came down the ramp. As long as that is the case we need to be prepared to cope with such invasions.

Battling the Ebola Virus

An illustration of CDC operations overseas was the campaign to identify an unknown and remarkably lethal infection that suddenly broke out in a Yambuku, a small village in the African nation of Zaire. At the same time CDC personnel were wrestling with the problem of Legionnaires disease in the civilized circumstances of Philadelphia, another team was fighting an even more malignant foe in the jungles of Africa. It was to become known as the Ebola Virus.

The first news of this outbreak came from European laboratories that had long established colonial contacts in the area. Even though the CDC has the necessary staff, experience, and specialized laboratories to deal with such emergencies, it cannot operate within other nations without an invitation from the government. As the emergency grew, and a second outbreak was identified in Sudan, personnel from the United States began to work on the problem.

It was a mystifying disease. The Sudan subtype had a fatality rate of 50%, which was terrifying enough. The Zairean variety had a fatality rate of 90%. A fatality rate like that could mean the end of a small village. Early studies indicated that the problem was some type of viral hemorrhagic fever, but which one was a mystery. Working with patients infected with the disease was extremely hazardous. Laboratory work had to be done in special labs to protect the scientists conducting the research. The devastating fever no one had seen before was named after the nearby Ebola river.

The disappointing aspect of this work is that no protective vaccine or effective antiviral drug has been found. As yet it is not even clear what the natural reservoir of the virus is. At the present time outbreaks of the virus are contained by isolating cases to prevent infection from one person to another and by rigid public health measures. At this point the National Institutes of Health began to work on the problem and have identified the protein that causes the internal bleeding which makes this virus so deadly. This is a major step toward developing a cure and a vaccine so it is likely that a cure is on the way.

The Epidemic Intelligence Service (EIS)

The EIS is an element of the CDC that helps it respond to outbreaks of disease both here and abroad. Each year from 60 to 80 health professionals are recruited for a two year post-graduate program of service and-on-the-job training in controlling epidemics. In the course of their service they may travel anywhere in the world to work with local officials in identifying outbreaks of dangerous diseases and working out systems of control.

Since this puts people who are interested in public health face to face with real life health emergencies backed up by the staff, the experience, and the facilities of the CDC, it is an extremely popular program. While non-citizens can apply, so many of the assignments are domestic only a few are accepted.

The Global AIDS Program (GAP)

The Centers for Disease Control has other programs that reach out to help other countries deal with threatening health problems. The current crisis in HIV-AIDS infections in many parts of the globe has led to the creation of a program with the obvious acronym GAP.

It is a cooperative arrangement negotiated with each government requesting assistance. GAP supplies money and technical assistance in setting up programs for controlling the spread of the disease, for education, and for assistance to individuals who have the disease and their families. At this time the GAP program is at work in 18 countries from Africa to Asia. Considering the enormous problems AIDS poses for these countries GAP can surely be considered a gift from America.

It is ironic, however, that the focus on the HIV/AIDS disaster has caused us to ignore other disastrous epidemics that have been with us far longer. Worldwide, Sexually Transmitted Disease (STD) infections are running over 400 million annually, one of the most under recognized health problems in the world. We seem to be leading the way. The National Center for HIV, STD, and TB Prevention reports that "In the United States more than 65 million people are living with an incurable sexually transmitted disease (STD). An additional 15 million people become infected with one or more STDs each years, roughly one half of whom contract lifelong infections."

In its 51 year history CDC has conducted more than 3,000 investigations of disease outbreaks including Legionnaire's disease, toxic shock syndrome, Reye's syndrome, Ebola, hemorrhagic fever, hantavirus, pulmonary syndrome and many foodborne and waterborne diseases. Their quick response teams have worked around the world aggressively investigating outbreaks of disease, identifying ways to stop transmission, and preventing further occurrence. The CDC has a great record of accomplishments but new challenges seem to arise every year. We can be very proud of this team and thankful that they are still on the job.

More Food for Everyone

Chapter 17

The United States Department of Agriculture

If you want to understand the full impact of the United States Department of Agriculture (USDA) on world food production you would have to be prepared for a long session. This is a venerable institution, 140 years old, founded when 58% of Americans were employed in farming. Today only 5% of Americans are employed in farming, in large measure the result of the department's long effort to reduce the physical labor in farming and increase productivity.

In its early days the USDA was involved in finding improved plant and animal varieties that could be adapted to our growing conditions. That is how the Washington navel orange came to California from Brazil, Durra sorghum came from Egypt, and winter wheat came to Kansas from Turkey. In time this came to be a two-way street and the USDA became a major international center for agricultural plant breeding, technology, and science. Its roster of research breakthroughs is far too large to fit in these pages. Selecting examples of activities that can unquestionably be considered gifts from America, is just a matter of picking a representative few. The only thing that complicates this choice is that so many of the department's contributions are known only within the agriculture industry. A new vaccine for hog cholera may be extremely important to hog farmers around the world and for the international food supply, but it won't get much attention from the news media.

As a consequence the few examples of the Department's achievements offered here were selected to show the range rather than the volume of its work.

The Penicillin Story

No, the USDA did not discover penicillin. Alexander Fleming, a Scottish bacteriologist, discovered this mold and it's astonishing power to kill bacteria. That discovery provided the medical profession with an incredible asset for dealing with infection, but only if someone could figure out how to produce the mold in large quantities. For more than ten years people suffered and died from common infections which could easily have been cured if only penicillin had been available.

In 1941 two scientists brought a sample of penicillin to this country from England hoping that experts here could devise an effective system of mass production to meet the needs of a nation at war. The project was assigned to Andrew Moyer, an expert in molds, at the USDA's Northern Laboratory in Peoria, Illinois. His first effort immediately increased yields ten times, but that didn't come close to meeting the need. So the search for improved production continued.

Ultimately, it was not new technology that solved the problem, but a superior strain of penicillin. Foraging through garbage cans in Peoria, the researchers found the strain they needed growing on a moldy cantaloupe. This was the breakthrough that led to true industrial production. The USDA didn't invent penicillin but it made the medicine available in the quantities needed for England's war effort and for the benefit of people all over the world. A nice gift. In the fight against disease you take your victories where you find them.

Subduing the Screwworm

It is hard to imagine a more disgusting form of infection than the attack of the screwworm, Cochliomyia hominivorax, on the living flesh of warm-blooded animals. The fly lays eggs in open sores or cuts and, as the eggs hatch, the larva use tusklike mandibles to consume the body of its animal host. An animal infected with screwworm shows pulsating blobs of larva busily digesting its flesh and growing to maturity so they can fly off to find another animal with an open sore.

Treating herd animals suffering from screwworms one by one was a slow process. In countries where cattle-raising was an important industry the screwworm was a serious economic problem. An alternative approach was needed.

Theoretically, if large batches of screwworm pupae were rendered sterile and introduced in the field to mate with fertile females the number of offspring would be greatly reduced. If this process were to be repeated over a period of time, the active population would be eliminated. Experiments conducted in Texas demonstrated that controlled amounts of x-radiation would make the screwworm pupae sterile without limiting its normal mating behavior. In short, sterile males mated normally but no offspring resulted.

Tests performed in Florida and the Netherland's Antilles confirmed the theory. The test consisted of releasing sterile flies by airplane each week. After nine weeks, no fertile eggs were found.

By 1966 the sterile-insect technique eliminated the screwworm problem in the United States. The campaign continued south of our border and in 1991 much of Central America and all of Mexico were declared free of screwworm.

This technology has been effective in controlling screwworm in other areas, most recently in Northern Africa, and may well be applied to control other insect populations. It has been a blessing in countries where it has been used successfully and may be a blessing in others in the future.

Choose Your Offspring, Male or Female

As research probes deeper into biological processes it begins to deal with problems that many people thought would never be touched. For more than ten years the USDA has been at work on a process to separate the sperm of farm animals, based on DNA content, into X-chromosome sperm producing females, and Y-chromosome sperm producing males.

In the field of animal husbandry the ability to make this distinction can have practical benefits. To produce fifty replacement calves for a dairy herd without separating sperm, one hundred cows would have to be bred, since approximately half the calves would be male. Artificially inseminating cows with X-chromosome sperm ensures that the calves dropped will be female and can be added to the milk producing herd.

The intriguing question is how to sort something that is so small that the naked eye can't see it. The process, developed by animal physiologist Lawrence Johnson, uses a fluorescent dye that adheres to sperm based on its DNA content. Female-producing sperm contains more DNA than male-producing sperm, so they can be separated by the amount of light they emit.

Like so many other advancements made in agricultural research the benefit is seen only by the farmer or herdsman. The wider benefit to the public would come from greater efficiency, better quality and better prices.

The ability to predetermine the sex of an offspring is an intriguing prospect to human beings. Apparently the Beltsville Sperm Sexing technology can be used for that purpose and the Department has licensed the technique to a private firm that is refining the process. The age old question "Boy or Girl" may soon be decided in advance. The ethical question in some minds is that while it may be all right for dairy cows is it all right for human beings?

Genetically Engineering Seeds for Superior Performance

Techniques that permit genes from other plants or life forms to be incorporated into seeds of agricultural crops makes it possible to create plants that have desirable characteristics they have never had before. For example this process makes it possible to create plants that have a built in resistance to insect attacks, a most desirable characteristic for most farmers.

While this process promises a new world of improved plants it is strongly opposed by some groups on the basis that we do not know what the long term effect of such changes will be on humans, animals, or the growing environment. Nevertheless, an increasing amount of the world's food is being grown using genetically altered seeds.

The USDA's Agricultural Research Service has been active in this field for a long time, doing basic research on the topic. They have created and patented a process for creating seeds that will produce plants that are resistant to insect attack. It applies not only to agricultural field crops but to fruit trees and ornamental plants as well. The great benefit of such crops is that they greatly reduce the need for spraying with agricultural chemicals.

There are other reasons for using genetic engineering to change crop characteristics. Soybeans, an extremely important crop worldwide, can cause severe allergic reactions among children and some adults. The Research Service estimates that 90% or more of food allergies are caused by soybeans and shellfish. Using a biotechnology method called "gene silencing" researchers have eliminated the allergen. In the future soybean products should cause fewer allergic problems for both children and adults.

The Research Service has patented a new variety of corn whose kernels hold less phytic acid. With less phytic acid animals with one stomach, humans, pigs, and chickens can absorb essential phosphorus from the grain they eat. Humans get most of their phosphorus from other elements in their diet but poultry and swine have always needed phosphorus supplements for healthy bone structure. An important side effect is that if the animals fed on low phytic acid corn absorb the phosphorus in their feed it will not be excreted as it is now. Phosphorus in manure is a serious pollution problem wherever animals are concentrated so low phytic acid corn can benefit hog and chicken breeders in two ways.

Helping Feed the World

In addition to extensive research programs that have contributed so much to improving world food production, the Department of Agriculture is a major participant in American Food Aid programs. The United States donates food under a several public laws, Public Law 480, also known as the Food for Peace law, Food for Progress and the Global Food for Education Initiative. The United States Agency for International Development is also involved in food distribution overseas. In the year 2001 U.S. food assistance totaled 6 million metric tons of which 4 million tons were provided by the Department of Agriculture.

Early in the year 2003 the USDA's Foreign Agricultural Service celebrated its 50th anniversary and was named at that time as the lead agency for implementing the new International Food for Education and Child Nutrition Program.

This new program will take over and build on the success of a pilot program, the Global Food for Education Initiative, that has been in operation for the past three years. The new program continues a commitment to improve the lives of children around the world, providing agricultural commodities for use in school feeding and pre-school nutrition projects in developing countries. Today it is estimated that 120 million children around the world do not attend school principally because of hunger and malnutrition. The vast majority of these children are young girls. During the past three years the program has been offered to 19 countries in Latin America, Africa, Asia, and Europe, distributing 485,375 metric tons of food with a value of 105 million dollars.

Because the program covers such a vast geographical area and must meet the special requirements of different countries and different cultures the Foreign Agricultural Service cooperates with a number of Non-Governmental Organizations (NGO's) who set up and operate the special programs for each country. The NGO's are permitted to sell part of the dry food received from the Foreign Agricultural Service in order to buy vegetables, fruit and other foods to provide a balanced diet.

Special attention is given in all the programs to encouraging girls to enroll and continue in school. In Pakistan where a serious effort is being made to increase the enrollment of girls, food is used as a strategy to get girls to attend. For a minimum of 20 days a month of school attendance each girl receives a ration of vegetable oil for her family. In Ghana a similar program is in effect. In Yemen 30,000 female students are given take-home rations of food three times a year. The effect of this program is not only to keep the girls involved in school, it also increases their status at home since they in effect become another bread-winner for the family.

Other food aid programs operate on a different basis. While USAID provides food aid directly in disaster situations, most food aid is negotiated with various governments to encourage them to take steps to improve economic development so that food aid can ultimately be phased out. As a USDA report on global food needs stated, "countries are not permanent wards of the food-aid system but graduate as their agriculture and economies improve." Egypt, Turkey, Indonesia, Sri Lanka, and Morocco, no longer receive food aid but have become important markets for agricultural products.

The Green Revolution and Norman Borlaug

One of the most prestigious honors the world community offers is the Nobel Peace Prize. What makes it so important is that it recognizes a contribution of great value to the world at large. The United States has had a number of winners of the Nobel Prize including such famous Americans as General George C. Marshall, who proposed the Marshall Plan and Dr Martin Luther King. Two other winners, Elie Weisel and Henry Kissinger, would also be known to many Americans but it is unlikely that many would have ever heard of Dr Norman Borlaug. It is even less likely that they would have ever heard of the Green Revolution, the agricultural breakthrough that improved food production in some of the world's poorest countries and that brought him this recognition.

129

Like so many advances in science and so much of the work done by the department the Green Revolution benefited from the contributions of a number of people, over a long period of time. In 1946 American agronomist Cecil Salmon, while serving in General Douglas MacArthurs headquarters in Japan, collected some strange looking wheat plants with short, stiff stems and heavy seed heads. One notable inclusion was labeled Norin No. 10. These plants were sent to a USDA seed repository and then redistributed to various wheat breeders.

A team of breeders at Washington State University, lead by Orville Vogel, worked with these imported varieties for thirteen years to develop a highly productive variety called Gaines. One of the visitors to the growing fields was Norman Borlaug of the International Maize and Wheat Research Center in Mexico. Borlaug was impressed with the short-stalked wheat's potential and the Washington State breeders shared their plant material with him.

The International Maize and Wheat Research Center was established by the Rockefeller Foundation and Norman Borlaug was selected to direct it. This was not considered an important post by American agronomists but Borlaug's focus and commitment turned it into one. While it was originally intended to teach Mexican farmers new methods, he expanded its mission to find new and more productive crops. His major achievement was the continued development of short-stemmed wheat, which was to become a crucial breakthrough for India and other nations.

In 1963 Norman Borlaug responded to an urgent request from the government of India to provide their plant breeders with short-stemmed wheat varieties. The new varieties, combined with improved cultural practices, enabled India to launch a true Green revolution, tripling its wheat production.

A similar sequence took place in the arid regions of India with the introduction of hybrid millet. In this case the work of USDA geneticist Glenn Burton provided the breakthrough by altering millet cytoplasm so it could be hybridized. In 1961 he sent sterile male millet seed to Indian plant breeders who used it to develop high-yield varieties for local use.

The full story of the green revolution is impressive. Since the new dwarf wheats were adaptable, they took hold in countries with similar growing conditions such as Pakistan, Turkey, and Afghanistan. They made dramatic improvements in food production in countries that were straining to feed their populations.

Norman Borlaug, who worked so hard to make these changes take place, may not be well known to the people in his own country but the results of his work are felt by people around the globe.

Research, Source of Future Gifts

Chapter 18

NASA, The Rocket People

When a huge rocket makes a dramatic departure from its base at Cape Canaveral, riding on a column of flame, it announces the fact with a roar that can be heard for miles and seen on television screens across America. It is the logo, the signature event, of the National Aeronautics and Space Administration.

Actually NASA embraces many other activities ranging from very pragmatic studies in aircraft operations to deep space explorations of the universe. Aerospace Technology Enterprises seeks improvements in all aspects of conventional aviation, Earth Science Enterprises studies the earth and its atmosphere, and Space Science Enterprises focuses on the solar system and deep space. With a current budget of 15 billion dollars it is one of this nation's primary agencies for research and pure science.

Aerospace Technology's mission is to make flying safer and more effective for everyone.

- Increase Safety by reducing the aircraft accident rate by a factor of five within ten years.
- Reduce emissions of exhaust gases by 70% within ten years.
- Reduce the perceived noise of future aircraft by a factor of two within 10 years

- Double the capacity of the aviation system within 10 years.

- Increase mobility by reducing inter-city door-to-door transportation time by half in 10 years.

The Earth Science Enterprise's mission is to develop a scientific understanding of the earth system, how it is changing, and the consequences of these changes for life on Earth.

- How is the global system changing?

- What are the primary forces on the Earth system?

- How does the Earth system respond to natural and human-induced changes?

- What are the consequences of change in the Earth system for human civilization?

- How well can we predict future changes in the Earth system?

In pursuit of this information NASA has recently launched the Earth Observing System Aqua satellite which will provide a six year chronology of our planet and its processes. It will allow scientists to assess long-term change, identify its human and natural causes and advance the development of models for long-term forecasting.

Aqua will also map the moisture content of soils all over the Earth's surface. This information will improve forecasts of rainfall, and other weather factors such as winds, temperature and humidity, critical factors for farmers all over the world.

While all of these activities are important, Space Science undertakes the most technically demanding projects in deep space. This enterprise currently has 31 Space Science missions operating and another 22 in development. These include such important assets in the field of astronomy as the Hubble Space Telescope and the Chandra X-ray Observatory.

Many of these projects take a long time to mature and are very expensive. The Cassini Mission is a good example. Loaded with sensitive instrumentation, Cassini will do a detailed study of the planet Saturn, its rings, its satellites, and its moon, Titan. Launched in 1997, the spacecraft won't get to Saturn until 2004. One of its missions is to deliver a probe to Titan provided by the European Space Agency. Understanding the nature of our solar system is a major scientific focus for nations around the world and this kind of cooperation with European and Japanese space agencies is normal.

So what "gifts" does NASA offer the world?

With thousands of talented scientists and engineers working on projects at the leading edge of knowledge we can reasonably expect some breakthroughs from NASA, even though some are incidental to the main thrust of their work. Here are some taken from NASA'S own list of important inventions.

- Bar Coding: Those narrow black lines frequently affixed to merchandise that can be scanned to ring up prices and keep track of inventory. Developed for keeping track of NASA's extremely complicated inventory of parts.

- Cordless Hand Tools: Battery powered hand tools that hang from the belts of construction workers and home-owners alike. Developed to expedite work in space.

- Fire Fighter's Equipment: New protective suits made of fire resistant fabric originally developed for use in space suits.

Many other are not seen by themselves but are incorporated in more complex applications.

- Complementary Metal-oxide Semiconductor Active Pixel Sensors or "Camera on a Chip." Incorporated in digital cameras and portable PC videophones.

- Phenylethynyl Terminated Imide Oligomers, fifth composition (Don't ask for this at the hardware store): A breakthrough in material science with exceptional properties that are important in aircraft applications.

The important work of NASA, however, remains in scientific inquiry that may take a long time to pay off. One long term project now being studied is the development of very large scale solar power systems in space and wireless transmission of the energy. The ultimate aim of this work is to utilize the boundless amounts of solar power available in space for use on earth. If this could be accomplished its practical value is obvious. It could be a gift of infinite value to planet earth.

In other projects, such as the Chandra X-ray Observatory, it is hard to find a practical payoff.

"It is performing an exploration of the hot turbulent regions in space with images 25 times sharper than previous x-ray pictures. Chandra's improved sensitivity will make possible more detailed studies of black holes, super novas, and dark matter and increase our understanding of the origin, evolution, and destiny of the universe."

No one could claim that this information is going to make life better on planet Earth in the foreseeable future. It is purely a pursuit of scientific knowledge. Yet, looking backwards through the centuries, we can see it is mankind's insatiable curiosity about the unknown that has provided what we now know about the world we live in. That will likely continue. Pure science is a gift that will payoff, but we can't know when that will happen.

Chapter 19

The Department of Energy

Chapter 8 covers the work of the National Renewable Energy Laboratory, a division of the Department of Energy (DOE) that deals with sources ranging from solar power to biomass, the use of farm wastes to generate power. But DOE is a very large agency, with a budget in excess of 20 billion dollars. It operates twenty five laboratories and research centers covering a wide range of subjects. Some of the world's most famous centers for advanced scientific research such as Brookhaven Laboratory, the Fermi National Accelerator, the Stanford Linear Accelerator and the Princeton Plasma Physics Laboratory operate under the Department of Energy.

Out of these laboratories has come a flood of technical and scientific knowledge. The Department provides long lists of these it considers to be important. Without questioning their ranking, combing those lists for jewels that would make sense to the layperson is slow work. Try this one. "Quantum dots, nanometer-size particles in which electrons are confined to a relatively small volume, have recently been shown to emit light at multiple wavelengths, blinking on and off on a time-scale of seconds." This may be a great breakthrough in our understanding of very small phenomenon and may have important benefits in the future but it is hard to see any immediate benefits flowing to the world from this knowledge.

Fortunately there are other advancements on the list that seem poised to bear fruit. In many cases these are achieved through collaboration between the DOE labs and commercial firms that contract to do part of the work.

- Oak Ridge National Laboratory devised an electric water heater that uses only one-third as much electricity as conventional water heaters through the use of a small drop-in heat pump. Researchers estimate that if one half of the nation's electric water heaters were replace by the new device our nation's entire energy consumption would be reduced by one percent.

- The National Renewable Energy Laboratory has developed a new solar cell, used for transforming the sun's energy to electricity. The new Triple-Junction cell converts as much as 34% of sunlight to electricity, 40% higher than its nearest competitor.

- The Ames Laboratory has developed a new reformer for converting standard fuels such as methanol, natural gas, or diesel to hydrogen. Much attention is now being focused on hydrogen-burning fuel cells to replace gasoline engines for future power needs. The new reformer is highly efficient, small in size, and quick acting, a significant improvement over other reformers.

- The Idaho National Engineering and Environmental Laboratory has developed a technique for spraying a Super Hard Steel Coating on metal surfaces. The process transforms steel alloy into a metallic glass coating which cannot be removed even with a hammer and chisel. It can be applied at lower cost than chrome plating or tungsten carbide.

- Brookhaven National Laboratory has developed a new technology for recovering silica from geothermal brine. Hot water from deep wells is a very useful source of energy for the production of electricity but the brine can be very hard on the processing equipment. The Brookhaven process not only improves the quality of the water but also produces high quality silica with many industrial applications.

The list could go on. The point is that the laboratories of the DOE are producing an endless stream of inventions, innovations, product improvements, and process improvements, designed to reduce costs, improve efficiency, increase the useful life of existing products or to introduce some new material that may have great benefits in ways we cannot now imagine. A recent breakthrough makes it possible to efficiently manufacture composite materials that mimic the construction of marine shells that provide hard, strong, tough shelters for fragile occupants. It is anticipated that this process will lead to materials with unprecedented properties.

143

While the breakthroughs listed are obviously of great benefit to the industrial and commercial world they may not seem to offer much to the developing world. But that is not the way these things work. If an improved plating technique produces a well pump that uses less power and the development of more efficient solar cells provide more power to remote communities, the developing world will benefit. The DOE clearly has gifts to offer everyone.

Far beyond these examples of applications research are those coming from the laboratories that deal with the nature of matter, research at the edge of our knowledge of the physical world. The topics these labs deal with and the language used in describing them are beyond the comprehension of most of us. Try determining the practical results of the following examples of work being done at the Brookhaven National Laboratory:

- "Ongoing experiments observing the decay of k mesons may reveal the first data incompatible with the Standard Model of particle physics"

- "Relativistic heavy Ion research into hot dense nuclear matter using the Alternating Gradient Synchroton Accelerator".

- "Fundamental discoveries in the demonstration of the existence of two kinds of neutrinos, of the Omega minus hyperon and of charm baryons."

Don't worry if you don't understand those activities. Very few people do.

Other laboratories deal with similar research and, since the facilities used for this kind of research are rare and extremely expensive, provide the base for students and scientists working at this level. The Fermi National Accelerator Laboratory serves 1,300 United States university scientists as well as 1,800 foreign users. Research at this level is international and American scientists have similar access to laboratories abroad.

These laboratories serve the world by participating in cutting edge research in the study of matter and by including researchers from other countries. When will this kind of work lead to benefits for humanity? No one can answer that but it could be tomorrow.

Chapter 20

The National Science Foundation, Funding Research

The NSF is a forty-year-old newcomer among Washington's science focused agencies. Impressed by the contributions science had made to the successful conclusion of World War II, political leaders undertook to insure continuing advancements in science and engineering by establishing a permanent organization to "promote the progress of science; to advance the national health, prosperity, and welfare; and to secure the national defense."

The foundation operates on a budget of $4.5 billion dollars through seven directorates covering fields from biological and information science to mathematical and social science. Through grants and contracts it supports scientific and engineering research. in all these fields. It also promotes education and awards graduate fellowships in these fields.

Its activities are wide ranging. It receives approximately 30,000 proposals each year for research, education, and training projects and funds about 10,000 of them. While NSF has no laboratories of its own, it does support some national research centers, oceanographic vessels, and Antarctic research centers.

Given the number of projects it supports it is not surprising that it has a broad geographical reach.

- One of the NSF's permanent research sites is in Antarctica where it studies long term climatic trends. While the overall temperature of the globe increased during the 20th century Antarctica has shown a decrease. Understanding the reason for this difference could be important in predicting future conditions around the world.

- Waters surrounding the continent of Antarctica support commercially valuable fisheries. In order to collect information about fish species in these waters and under the ice sheets NSF has conducted research using trained Weddell seals equipped with cameras and data recorders to observe these species. The use of marine predators as guided, high-speed sampling devices has provided new information about species that have been especially difficult to study.

- NSF has funded a dig at Blombos Cave in South Africa that has excavated artifacts over 70,000 years old covered with abstract representations. This discovery indicates that human beings were capable of abstract thinking much earlier than had previously realized.

- It sponsors a project taking core samples from the bottom of Lake Malawi in the East African Rift Valley, one of the worlds oldest and deepest lakes, that will greatly expand our knowledge of early climatic history. Sediments retrieved from the bottom of the lake, which is more than 700 meters deep and more than seven million years old are expected to reveal important data about the evolution of Earth's climate.

The geographic spread of NSF-funded research is exceeded only by the range of subject matter covered. Some of these projects have very practical objectives, while others involve pure rather than applied research. Some of the pure research reveals fascinating new knowledge whose application may not be apparent now but in time may be extremely beneficial.

- One intriguing project supported by the NSF has produced a new class of materials called "left-handed", because in response to electromagnetic radiation they reverse many of the characteristics of normal materials. Sheldon Schultz, one of the physicists leading this research says "If these effects turn out to be possible at optical frequencies, this material would have the crazy property that a flashlight shining on a slab can focus the light at a point on the other side."

- A more pragmatic series of grants funded by the NSF and the EPA will study the use of plants for phytoremediation of soils contaminated by heavy metals or organic chemicals. Contaminated soils are a serious problem world-wide, affecting human health, ecosystems, and agriculture. This research will find and develop plants that degrade, remove, or stabilize toxic compounds from contaminated soil and water. The use of plants to correct these problems could be extremely cost-effective and much less disruptive than traditional techniques, such as moving contaminated soil to hazardous waste landfills.

The history of science supports the idea that fundamental research pays off in ways that are not immediately apparent. When physicist I.I. Rabi first described the principle of the atomic clock it was not at all clear what useful purpose such an incredibly accurate clock could serve. Today it is the essential element in The Global Positioning System, the set of satellites that makes it possible to instantly determine your location anywhere on the surface of the earth.

Another breakthrough in 1946 revealed the phenomenon called nuclear magnetic resonance. Few would have predicted when Stanford and Harvard researchers discovered this phenomenon that the study of the spin characteristics of basic matter would lead in the 1970s to improvements in health care. Today, it is the basis for Magnetic Resonance Imaging (MRI) equipment that can detect tumors and investigate brain tissue, and is in wide use in the medical field.

In the course of providing funding for important research the NSF has supported about half of the U.S. Nobel laureates in the major fields of science and about 60% of the 30 Nobel Laureates in economics. Considering the breakthroughs in understanding that these prizes represent, NSF has clearly been putting support in the right places.

The NSF has supported applied research that has been of great value to the world, a true gift from America. It has also supported work that may be hard to evaluate now but could be of great value in the future.

Chapter 21

A Treasure of Nobel Laureates

When Alfred Nobel, the Swedish inventor of dynamite, died in 1896 he left a considerable estate to endow prizes in the fields of science, literature, and the cause of world peace. Since that time the Nobel Prizes have grown in stature to become the world's most prestigious recognition of individual merit in those fields.

This is especially true of the three awards in the field of science, Physics, Chemistry and Physiology or Medicine. At the beginning of the last century when the first awards were made, awards in these three categories were dominated by scientists and physicians in the nations of Western Europe. In recent years this dominance has changed. It is now the United States that is the largest recipients of Nobel Awards in science.

In the years from 1940 to 1998 a total of 333 Nobel Prizes were awarded in Physics, Chemistry and Physiology and Medicine. This number is greater than the number of years involved because the awards are frequently split into two or three to recognize that several people may have contributed to a particular scientific breakthrough. Of that number, 203 awards, 61% of the total, were made to individuals who were doing their research in the United States.

Before we rejoice too much over those numbers we should look at another set of figures. While 61% of the Prizes were awarded to individuals working in the United States, 29% of those individuals came to the United States from some other country. With the tremendous research establishment and the funding sources available here we make it possible for some highly talented people to come here and continue studies they might not have been able to carry out in their own country.

Looking through the list of Nobel Awards given to people in this country you quickly grasp what an awesome research establishment we have here. All of the leading universities are represented with multiple awards. Other institutions such as Bell Labs, Rockefeller Institute, Mayo Clinic, and the Salk Institute represent just a fraction of the places where serious, advanced scientific work is being done. Looming over all with money and facilities to keep this activity going are the National Institutes of Health, the National Science Foundation, NASA, and the Department of Energy. The National Institutes of Health have supported the work of 97 scientists who have won Nobel Prizes. Five of them have made their prize winning discoveries while working in the NIH Laboratories. All five Nobel Laureates for 1998, three in physics and two in chemistry, received funding from the National Science Foundation.

The National Science Foundation has a similar record in the Nobel awards in Economics. Sixty percent of the 30 Nobel Laureates in economics have received support from the Foundation.

Making it possible for talented scientists to come to this country and continue their work is a gift of great value. At the same time it is a process that benefits us greatly. We should hope that all of our gifts are so mutually beneficial.

Other Gifts from Other Sources

Chapter 22

The Remarkable Non-Governmental Organizations

Benefits flow from the United States to other parts of the world in a variety of ways. Not all of them are connected with the United States Government. American residents send billions of dollars each year to their families in other countries. In some countries these remittances form a major part of their foreign exchange income. But these payments represent private, person to person, charity and can't be considered gifts from the American people

The NGO's are in a different category. They are voluntary, non-profit groups organized to provide services and humanitarian functions on an international basis. The American Council for Voluntary International Action, "InterAction", has over one hundred and sixty members operating in over 100 countries. The names of many members such as the American Friends Service Committee, the American Red Cross, CARE, and Save the Children, are familiar in our country as well as overseas.

The range of activities of "Interaction" members is startling. While some NGO's are very large, with complex operations in a number of countries dealing with women's rights, health, the environment, refugees, and disaster relief, others send retired executives overseas to help the development of small businesses, provide livestock for poor farmers, and distribute solar cookers in areas that have exhausted their local fuel supplies. Many religious groups are represented. And there are others. The ability of Americans to find solutions to problems in the international field seems unlimited. If a corporation finds itself with more of last years model than it really wants, someone will figure out how to move that surplus to places in the world that really need it. In fact, someone has. Its name is Gifts in Kind International. It is called product philanthropy.

NGO's raise money from a variety of sources for their operations and also contract with our government to provide specific services in disaster areas. A good way to see how these organizations function is to look at their operations in the Sudan.

The Sudan has been the scene of an intractable, continuous, long term, man-made human disaster. The participation of the United States Agency for International Development in the Sudanese disaster is discussed in Chapter 3. The scale of the problems there is such that a lot of agencies are involved including ten NGO's.

These NGO's contract to provide specific humanitarian services and developmental activities in specific regions of that war-torn country. They provide experienced staff and train local people to help them carry out their responsibilities.

Save The Children is focused on the lives of disadvantaged women and children. During the past seventy years it has operated in over forty countries in the developing world to help children and families improve their health, education, and economic opportunities.

The Sudan Field Office of Save the Children has several operations in the Kordofan region of the Sudan. Their services range from the provision of primary survival needs to developing self-sustaining communities. In one of their programs, involving 154,000 people, they manage food aid distribution, support sanitary water supplies by rehabilitating village wells, enhance food security by providing seeds and tools, and providing goats to families headed by women.

Their activities are varied. At one end of the scale they cover school construction and rehabilitation, provision of school supplies, teacher training, and support for extra curricular activities in 30 target village sites. At the other end they sponsor village water supply activities by digging reservoirs for rain water harvesting.

The American Refugee Committee has, for twenty years, focused on the survival, health, and well-being of refugees, displaced persons, and those at risk. The countries where they have operated in the past twenty years reads like a list of international trouble spots around the world, Bosnia, Croatia, Kosovo, Macedonia, Rwanda, Thailand, and, of course, the Sudan.

The ARC has been in operation in Kajo Keji County in the Sudan since 1994, providing an integrated program of primary healthcare and sanitation for refugees and displaced people. They currently support 11 Primary Health Care Units and 2 Primary Health Care Centers serving the 112,000 people in this area all staffed with local Sudanese that have been trained by ARC. Their purpose is to create an environment here that is conducive to the voluntary repatriation of Sudanese refugees from Uganda.

CARE is one of the world's largest private international relief and development organizations. Since its founding in 1945 it has become a leader in sustainable development and emergency aid, reaching tens of millions of people each year in 60 countries in Africa, Asia, Europe, and Latin America.

CARE has a long history in the Sudan, beginning operations in North Sudan in 1979 and in South Sudan since 1994. What began with emergency relief efforts has evolved to include development and rehabilitation programs focusing on agricultural, environmental and primary health care facilities serving 1.5 million people.

CARE's work covers a wide range of activities. From providing emergency water services to big refugee camps caring for 138,00 displaced persons to building permanent institutions in the form of farmer's marketing cooperatives to help develop food security in the Southern Sudan, the task of rebuilding the Sudan seem endless.

The agencies listed above work at the grass roots level in parts of the country that have been devastated by years of conflict. Part of their mission is to employ and train local people. Their reports express their constant concerns about the political instability of certain parts of the country and the physical safety of their staffs. It is an exceedingly difficult environment for carrying on humanitarian activities.

The contracts with USAID'S Office of Foreign Disaster Assistance are tailored to meet specific needs in specific areas and to cope with emergencies in the form of floods, droughts, or cholera epidemics as they arise. It is hard to see how these complex problems could be dealt with if the NGO's were not there.

The organizations working in the Sudan operate in many other parts of the world. They have the experience, the resources, and the staff to take on the complex assignments they are managing in the Sudan at the same time they are running similar programs in other countries. They are an invaluable resource. However, they are not the whole NGO story. There are other NGO's that also operate around the world but in a highly focused, specialized, manner.

The International Executive Service Corps (IESC) draws on a database of 12,000 seasoned executives willing to volunteer to take on-site consulting assignments and mentoring for both private and governmental enterprises in countries that lack the necessary expert knowledge. Each year these experts help hundreds of businesses and institutions in more than 50 countries. The range of their activities is impressive.

- Hans Lauer, the former supervising chef for Hilton Hotels, had already completed 36 food-related projects for IESC when a group of Bulgarian Hotels asked him to train their chefs. They wanted to improve their food services in hopes of increasing their share of the tourist market. Chef Lauer conducted a three week training course in food and beverage management, service and guest relations and motivation and leadership.

- Edward Culhane, volunteer expert on quality systems, in three separate assignments helped a Russian defense contractor shift its activities from aerospace to hearing aids. By improving the quality of its products the company not only expanded its sales in Russia, it became an exporter of high quality parts to manufacturers in other countries.

- In Zambia IESC has assembled a team of twelve volunteers working with 82 enterprises to help the city of Livingstone increase its appeal to tourists. The city sits on the banks of the Zambezi River and provides the best view of the mile wide, 400 foot high Victoria Falls. Through workshops and seminars the volunteers defined the kind and quality of services that would be needed to appeal to international travelers. The training started with such basic requirements as accurate record keeping and went on to management and market planning.

In addition to its seasoned business executives IESC has a new division called the "Geekcorps". The "Geekcorp" recruits younger volunteers who have expert knowledge in computer networks, communication systems, and internet web site designs. Volunteers are already helping businesses in Africa, Central Asia, the Middle East and Eastern Europe.

Heifer International has been providing dairy animals and other livestock to impoverished communities around the world to help them become self sufficient since 1944. They currently have 238 projects underway in 48 countries. Since they work in such diverse areas the kind of livestock they provide varies greatly, from dairy cows and dairy goats to water buffalo, yaks, llamas, and alpacas. If those don't work you may get sheep, rabbits, chickens, or guinea pigs. You will also get expert instructions in how to manage the livestock gifts.

Since some impoverished communities have devastated their physical environments Heifer International has found it necessary to expand its offerings to include trees and grass seeds that can be used to stabilize soil and develop new pasture areas for the expanded livestock herds.

Basic to the Heifer International concept is that every individual who receives a livestock gift must pass on one of the offspring to someone else. Over time this spreads the benefits of the original gift.

- The need for designing special programs to suit special needs is shown by looking at a few of the 238 projects that are currently underway. Following a disastrous winter in southeast China, Heifer International assisted 2000 disaster victims in desperate need of help. They were provided with 1,000 yaks, 500 dairy cows, 5,000 goats, and 500 beef cattle. They were also provided with tree and grass seedlings, and expert training, to repair the damage done by the storms.

- A project serving 165 families affected by leprosy in Thailand has an unusual mix of supplies. They will receive 175 cattle, 30 water buffalo, 50 pigs, 1,300 chickens, and 10,000 fingerling fish. In addition they will receive 1,000 fruit trees, four units of grasshoppers, two sheets of silk worms, three bamboo handicraft machines, and 8,820 pounds of animal feed.

- Flexibility helps in dealing with poverty problems around the world. In 2000, the Maasai people of northern Tanzania, successful herders for centuries, found that many of their cattle perished in the extreme drought. Supplying them with more heifers who would surely die under these hostile conditions wouldn't solve anything. What saved them was the introduction of camels, animals they had never seen before. Shifting from cattle herding to camel herding would have been a cultural problem under normal circumstances but not under drought conditions.

Solar Cookers International offers help in parts of the world where the landscape has essentially been stripped of fuel wood, a common problem in arid areas. Their program makes solar cookers available in such areas and provides the training to make their use safe and effective.

- Solar cookers are devices that reflect and focus the sun's heat on a cooking utensil. They range from simple parabolic mirrors for single family use to more complex units that track the sun's path across the sky and can provide cooking time for a small community. In doing this they spare the vegetation in the area, save the animal dung that would otherwise be burned so that it can be applied to the soil as fertilizer, and save the cost of kerosene or other liquid fuels. Solar cookers can make a real difference in areas where the principal resource is sunshine.

- Solar cookers offer another considerable benefit by providing a source of safe drinking water. Solar Cookers International estimates that worldwide, about 1.3 billion people do not have access to safe drinking water and that an estimated 1.5 billion cases of diarrhea each year result in the deaths of 2 million children. Boiling the water in a solar cooker solves this problem but their figures indicate that an easier solution pasteurizes it by holding the water at 150 degrees for five minutes.

Accion International addresses an entirely different problem, fighting poverty by making small loans that permit individuals to start businesses of their own. These loans may provide the capital that enables people with no resources to open a stall in the market, buy a loom, a potter's wheel, or a sewing machine, and begin to work for themselves. This process is called microlending. Such loans may be as small as $100, loans that regular banks have little interest in.

Accion International works with more than twenty five partner organizations that offer microfinance services to the poor in the countries of Latin America, the Caribbean, and sub-Saharan Africa. Because these borrowers frequently have no collateral or co-sponsors they may be teamed up with other borrowers in solidarity groups in which the members guarantee each others loans in lieu of collateral. Like any form of banking, microlending won't work unless the loans are repaid so that funds are available for other borrowers. Over the past decade the programs and partners affiliated with Accion International have made 3.8 billion dollars in microloans to 2.3 million people with a historical repayment rate of 97%.

Whether the microloan enables a wife to add some income to the family resources or starts an enterprise involving the whole family, it can mean a better life for some people who have no other way out of poverty.

Gifts In Kind International started in 1983 as a result of a corporate product donation from 3M Corporation. Today top manufacturers and retailers, including 40% of the Fortune 500 companies rely on Gifts in Kind to design and manage the donation process. In 2001 Gifts in Kind International and its 350 global affiliates distributed more than 675 million dollars in quality products to a network of more than 50,000 charitable nonprofits around the world.

Only registered and approved charitable non-profits can participate in this program but once they are approved they have a remarkable array of goods and services available to them, ranging from outright gifts to substantial discounts on first line products. The names of the companies offering donations or discounts includes many of the Blue Chip stars in American industry, IBM Corporation, Cisco Systems, Hewlett Packard, Motorola, Kodak, Seagate Technology, and a host of others. Registered members of Gifts in Kind can click on the roster of participating corporations to find the donations currently on offer.

This program is an obvious blessing to charitable non-profits and makes it easy for corporations to be charitable themselves.

The NGO's mentioned in this chapter are only a fraction of those who are making a great contribution to solving problems of poverty, health, education, and social justice around the world. It is surprising that this group of international benefactors is so little known and receives so little recognition for their work. They operate in many parts of the world and cooperate with many agencies to accomplish their humanitarian goals. The Department of Defense has helped them by airlifting tons of food, clothing, and medicines to foreign sites They raise money for their own operations through fund raising activities like any charitable non-profit. The budgets for the members of Interaction total almost six billion dollars of which approximately one billion comes from U.S. Government grants and contracts

That leaves a total of five billion that these NGO's collect from members, dues, grants from foundations, contributions in kind, and other sources. Since those funds come principally from the American people it seems reasonable to include the work of the NGO's as an important part of America's gifts.

The Index

About the Author

Cornelius Deasy is a retired Fellow of the American Institute of Architects now living in San Luis Obispo, California. He has been honored by the National Endowment for the Arts for his work showing the effect of design on human behavior and with design awards for his building projects. Two previous books "Design for Human Affairs and "Designing Places for People" deal with this work.

Gifts From America is the author's rebuttal to those who claim that the United States treats the world with arrogance and greed. It spells out our country's long time record as a generous citizen of the world, a record Americans have every right to be proud of.

www.ingramcontent.com/pod-product-compliance
Lightning Source LLC
Chambersburg PA
CBHW020415290526
45785CB00002B/572